CW00338707

AN ILLUSTRATED ENCYCLOPEDIA OF
BATTLESHIPS
FROM 1860 TO THE FIRST WORLD WAR

AN ILLUSTRATED ENCYCLOPEDIA OF
BATTLESHIPS
FROM 1860 TO THE FIRST WORLD WAR

More than 200 archive and museum photographs

Peter Hore

southwater

This book is dedicated to my daughter, Eleanor.

This edition is published by Southwater, an imprint of Anness Publishing Ltd, Blaby Road, Wigston, Leicestershire LE18 4SE; info@anness.com

www.southwaterbooks.com; www.annesspublishing.com

Anness Publishing has a new picture agency outlet for images for publishing, promotions or advertising. Please visit our website www.practicalpictures.com for more information.

Publisher: Joanna Lorenz
Project Editor: Lucy Doncaster
Copy Editor: Tim Ellerby
Designer: Ian Sandom
Cover Designer: Balley Design
Production Controller: Wendy Lawson

© Anness Publishing Ltd 2012

All rights reserved. No part of this publication may be reproduced, stored in a retrieval system, or transmitted in any way or by any means, electronic, mechanical, photocopying, recording or otherwise, without the prior written permission of the copyright holder.

A CIP catalogue record for this book is available from the British Library.

Previously published as part of a larger volume, *Battleships*

PUBLISHER'S NOTE
Although the advice and information in this book are believed to be accurate and true at the time of going to press, neither the authors nor the publisher can accept any legal responsibility or liability for any errors or omissions that may have been made.

PAGE 1: *Hood*
PAGES 2–3: *General Admiral Graf Apraksin*
PAGE 4: *Maine*
PAGE 5: **The Duncans**

Contents

Introduction

A basic style of sailing ship, capable of taking its place in the line of battle, or a "line-of-battle ship", from which the term battleship is derived, had dominated warfare at sea from the 16th to the 19th century. Then, just as the British navy delivered the victory of sea power in 1805 at the Battle of Trafalgar, new technology became available, which would revolutionize battleship design.

This revolution encompassed the use of steam engines at sea, breech-loading guns, the rotating turret, armour and above all the increase in size of ships. At one stage a British prime minister complained that ship design was a changing fashion like ladies' hats. There were developmental dead ends as well. The paddle ship with its exposed wheels was useless as a vehicle of war; the paddlewheels and boxes were too vulnerable to damage and restricted the size of broadside armament that could be mounted. However, the paddle ship was useful for towing sailing ships into action.

Other lines of development took unexpected turns. The monitor was designed for coastal defence and for war in the estuaries and rivers, and was highly successful in the American Civil War. However, when given a little more sea-keeping capability, the monitors became a powerful weapon of offence, mounting some of the largest guns, taken from their "big sister" battleships. In two world wars monitors were used in operations from the Arctic to Africa, and indeed at the end of their lives the shore-bombardment role of some battleships could be compared to that of an over-large monitor. In this

TOP: **USS *Merrimac* engages USS *Monitor*.** ABOVE: **HMS *Warrior* was so strongly built that she has survived until today. She has been beautifully restored and can be seen in Portsmouth, England.**

sense the monitor stands in line with the development of the cruise and ballistic missiles launched from submarines.

The battleship itself, broadly defined here as a capital ship mounting guns of 255mm/10in calibre or more, took on many different shapes for the first 20 years of its life as a distinct species. Designers faced difficult choices, weight being a primary factor in the decisions which had to be made. Many early designs had large, heavy barbettes which meant a low freeboard and loss of sea-keeping – the alternative was a high-sided ship with a consequent loss of stability. This period was marked by some exceedingly odd and ugly ships.

By the end of the 19th century the design of the battleship had more or less settled on a ship of about 10,160 tonnes/ 10,000 tons carrying two twin barbettes or turrets, one forward and one aft, sometimes with side-by-side funnels, and a speed

TOP: *Rhode Island*, with her superimposed turrets, became a veteran of the Great White Fleet. ABOVE: This French ship was a member of the Danton class, comprised of the first large turbine-engine ships, and which had large batteries of rapid-fire tertiary guns. ABOVE LEFT: A British battleship in dry dock showing her enormous bulbous ram. This line of development came about as a result of incorrect analysis of the Battle of Lissa in 1866.

of 18 knots was considered fast. At this point, the British admiral, Jacky Fisher, changed everything with his concept of a battleship which would "dread nought". It was not his idea alone. The Italian naval engineer Vittorio Cuniberti's proposals for an all-big-gun ship were widely published and there were simultaneous developments in the same direction in several other countries, as well. However, it was Fisher's energy, enthusiasm and drive which brought the first ship, HMS *Dreadnought* into being, and halted warship-building worldwide while friends and rivals considered what had been achieved. Although the design was not perfect, the ship was revolutionary in nearly every respect and thereafter battleships had to be classified by reference to this one ship: pre-Dreadnoughts, Dreadnoughts or super-Dreadnoughts. Thus the advent of HMS *Dreadnought* brought the early phase of battleship development to a close and retrospectively designated it as pre-Dreadnought.

There were only two large-scale fleet actions involving this type: the Battle of Lissa in 1866, involving a mixture of ironclads and wooden warships on both sides, and the Battle of Tsushima in 1905 between pre-Dreadnoughts. Other historically significant engagements of this period include the coastal bombardment of Russian shore positions by armoured batteries and steam warships at Kinburn in the Crimea, and the inconclusive duel between USS *Monitor* and CSS *Virginia* (formerly *Merrimac*) during the American Civil War.

This book looks at the fascinating history of the pre-Dreadnought battleship, from the first broadside ironclads of the mid-19th century through to the eve the development of the Dreadnought. It also describes the main battles and naval operations mounted by the world's foremost naval powers, notably Britain, the United States, Germany, France, Italy and Japan. The country-by-country chronological directory that follows describes the most famous pre-Dreadnought ships. This then is the story, told through the lives of individual ships, of the development, deployment and demise of the early types of battleship, which ultimately led to the development of the *Dreadnought* and the modern battleship.

The History of Pre-Dreadnoughts

The term "battleship" derives from "line-of-battle ship", meaning a ship strong enough to fight in the line of battle – but there was confusion of nomenclature. *Warrior,* laid down in 1859, was certainly the strongest ship of her time, yet she was never officially a battleship, only a frigate (because of her single gun deck), although she was later rated an armoured cruiser. The French called all the new battleships that developed in the later 19th century and the early 20th century *cuirassé*, and the Spanish called them *acorazado*, but these terms concentrated on the protective nature of armour. When the Germans came to build their navy they were more precise, using the terms *linienschiff, panzerschiff, schlachtschiff* and *schlachtkreuzer* to indicate different waypoints in the development of the battleship. The British navy began to re-introduce the term "battleship" around 1880 to mean a recognizable type of ship that was heavily armed and armoured. As technology advanced with the advent of steam, with propellers, breech-loading guns, turret mountings, turbines, armour plating, gun propellant and explosive power, so the modern battleship evolved.

LEFT: **The Japanese pre-dreadnought *Asahi*, here seen at anchor in Portsmouth in 1900. Built in Britain, she was sister ship to *Mikasa*, Admiral Togo's flagship at the decisive Battle of Tsushima, and was also present at the battle.**

LEFT: **The Crimean War was in fact a campaign and part of a larger war, more accurately known as the Russian War 1854–6, which raged on a global scale, and depended heavily upon sea power as this crowded anchorage in the Crimea shows.**
BELOW: **For an attack upon Kinburn, the French navy devised some armoured box-like ships, just visible through the smoke, with which they could approach the low-lying Russian fortifications. These craft, which were little more than rafts, are generally considered the genesis of the modern battleship.**

The Russian War

By the time of the Russian War of 1854–6, all the ingredients for a revolution in battleship design and construction were in place. Steam propulsion had been successfully applied at sea to a large number of paddle ships, and shortly thereafter many wooden walls had been converted to screw-steam propulsion. British shipyards were proficient in building iron hulls, armour was beginning to be applied to warships and guns were increasing in killing-power.

The actual impetus for the development of the battleship grew out of the campaign in the Black Sea, which is sometimes erroneously known as the Crimean War after the peninsular on which the famous land battles such as Balaclava, Inkerman, Alma and the siege of Sevastopol took place. The combined force of the British and French fleets, which arrived in the Black Sea in March 1854 to protect Ottoman shipping and ensure the lines of supply for the land-based expeditionary forces, were massively superior to any force that the Russians were able to put to sea. The problem faced by the allies was, therefore, how to take the war to their opponents.

Elsewhere, a naval expedition to the Baltic Sea constituted part of the broader offensive against Russia in 1854, although it achieved very little. The expedition was poorly planned, with little intelligence gathering prior to the opening of hostilities. Information regarding the strength and disposition of the fortifications of the Baltic coast was almost non-existent, and most of the ships assigned to the campaign had too heavy a draft to be useful for inshore work in a shallow sea, something

that may have influenced the decision to build so many coastal bombardment vessels later on. The fleet had to satisfy itself with the capture of merchant ships and blockading Russian ports, although the fortress of Bomarsund in the Åland Islands was stormed and captured by 10,000 French troops. In 1855, a second expedition bombarded the fortress of Sveaborg, near Helsingfors (Helsinki), although the ships' ordnance were to prove completely ineffective against the impressive walls of Cronstadt. At the other extremity of the Russian Empire, minor naval operations took place off the coast of Kamchatka, in the far east, and there was also some offensive action in the White Sea, although none of these had any influence over the outcome of the fighting in the Black Sea theatre of operation.

In November 1853 a Russian fleet had destroyed a squadron of Turkish frigates at Sinope using shell fire, and following the action had reportedly cleared wounded sailors from the stricken Ottoman vessels using grapeshot, an act that caused widespread condemnation and that lent much support to the pro-war lobby. Another more military-minded observer, Louis Napoleon III, who considered himself an artillery expert, proposed that floating shellproof batteries should be created to deal with the threat and for attacking the coast.

The technology of the time was just about to produce 100mm/4in armour plate, which was tested independently in Britain and France in order to construct a number of batteries with armour which fitted together with tongue-and-groove joints and was bolted to the hull. The resulting vessels were scarcely manoeuvrable under their own steam power and were unwieldy under sail, which meant that they had to be towed for most of their passage.

In 1855, three French armoured batteries saw action at Kinburn in the Crimea, where, in flattery to the Emperor, they were credited with destroying Russian shore positions. A more realistic assessment is that the low-lying Russian earthworks were actually flattened by mortar- and bomb-fire and from being blasted at close range by the accompanying battleships. Nevertheless, Kinburn saw the first use of armoured steam warships in battle.

The British took this basic idea a step further and built an immense fleet of gunboats and mortar vessels with which to attack St Petersburg. These were specifically designed to operate in the shallow waters of the Baltic Sea, thus placing the fortresses and cities that had eluded them in the first campaign well within their destructive range. In the event, the

news of this fleet alone was sufficient to bring the Tsar to the negotiating table, once again demonstrating the ability of the Royal Navy to project British power abroad and act as a deterrent to further conflict. This position was further underlined when, on St George's Day 1856, the Royal Navy organized a review of their fleet to remind the rest of the world of its power.

Such an overt display of naval prowess naturally provoked reactions among the other major powers of the time, particularly in Europe. Indeed the war was no sooner over than France began to devise ways of designing a ship that could challenge the Royal Navy, reawakening the historical rivalry that had been put aside during the Russian conflict. This resulted in Dupuy de Lôme designing the first seagoing ironclad, *Gloire,* a vessel that caused great concern in Britain.

Utilizing the production and shipbuilding capabilities of the greatest industrialized nation of the time, the British quickly countered with the iron-framed *Warrior* and *Black Prince.* These seagoing ironclads were significantly superior to the *Gloire* – their iron frames making for a much stronger construction, greater length and a correspondingly greater number and weight of guns – and their launch allowed the Royal Navy to re-established its supremacy.

BELOW: **The cattle pier at Balaclava. Supply by sea was critical to the land-based expeditionary forces of France, Britain and Turkey. The British established their base at Balaclava and eventually built a light railway to bring supplies up to the siege lines outside the heavily fortified Russian-held port of Sevastopol.**

Swedish influences in the United States Navy

The lessons of the Russian War and developments in warship design were noted in the USA where three Swedes – Ericsson, Fox and Dahlgren – strongly influenced the early United States Navy (USN).

John Ericsson had been an engineer in the Swedish Army when he moved to Britain in 1826 to sell his ideas (not all of them successful) for steam engines, screw propellers, large guns and even engines driven by hot air instead of steam.

In 1839 Ericsson was recruited to work in the USA, where, with Robert Stockton, he designed the heavily armed screw-driven USS *Princeton*. In 1843 an explosion in one of *Princeton*'s guns, an accident for which Ericsson's design was blamed, killed the US Secretary of State and the Secretary of the Navy. This scapegoating, in conjunction with the disintegration in the relationship between Ericsson and Stockton, led to Ericsson's acrimonious departure from the USN for a career in civil engineering.

After the outbreak of the American Civil War, Ericsson, spurred on by the development of *Virginia*, designed and built a revolutionary armoured ship – *Monitor* – which carried her guns in a rotating turret. This, like many of his designs, was a novel but not entirely successful initiative. Active until his death at age 83, Ericsson continued to produce ideas for submarines, self-propelled torpedoes and heavy ordnance.

John Dahlgren was the son of the Swedish consul in Philadelphia, who after some years in the USN started work in the Washington Navy Yard, helping to found the USN's ordnance department. Here he designed the Dahlgren gun, a range of weapons of three main types – bronze boat howitzers and rifles, iron smoothbores, and iron rifles.

His first weapons were adopted by the USN in 1850. These 12- and 24-pounder bronze pieces were primarily designed for use on small launches, but most vessels were to carry them during the American Civil War. His iron smoothbore cannon became the standard weapon of the Union navy during the Civil War and was known as the Dahlgren gun. The 229mm/9in smoothbore was adopted in 1850 and the 280mm/11in 1851.

The ironclad Monitor class mounted two of these guns in their turrets. However, as a result of an accidental explosion of a Dahlgren gun during testing in 1860, the USN insisted upon significantly reducing the levels of propellant powder used. This constraint inevitably resulted in diminished fire power, a factor that reportedly prevented USS *Monitor* from being able to destroy CSS *Virginia*. In 1862, the 381mm/15in Dahlgrens superseded the 229mm/9in and 280mm/11in weapons.

BELOW: **The USN continued to build low-freeboard monitors and to make trans-Atlantic crossings until the 20th century: here a US monitor passes a high-sided broadside French ship, herself a survivor from an earlier age.**
RIGHT: **One of the first acts of the newly pacified USA was to send a naval mission to Europe led by the Secretary of the Navy Gustavus Fox, in the un-seaworthy-looking monitor *Miantonomoh*.**

In 1863, John Dahlgren commanded the South Atlantic Blockading Squadron and saw his guns in action at Charleston. As the Civil War ended, Dahlgren – now a rear admiral – was assigned responsibility for the development and design of a range of boat howitzers, some of which were rifled, and an extensive range of other rifled ordnance. In 1869, he rejoined the Washington Navy Yard, where he worked until his death.

Gustavus Vasa Fox retired after nearly 20 years in the USN. In the American Civil War, after volunteering to command an expedition to relieve the garrison at Fort Sumter, Fox was appointed chief clerk of the Department of the Navy and then Assistant Secretary of the Navy, where his honesty and efficiency were much needed. In this capacity Fox effectively became the chief of naval operations. He kept in touch personally with senior officers and planned many of the navy's campaigns against the Confederacy. Fox was also a keen advocate of new technology – including Ericsson's Monitor.

In mid-1866 Fox crossed the Atlantic in the monitor *Miantonomoh*, demonstrating the sea-worthiness of a low-freeboard, armoured turret ship. Fox visited northern Europe, including Russia, and the officers of his squadron used the opportunity to collect naval intelligence. However, Fox soon resigned from office to enter business. The USN went into a decline that lasted for the next few decades, and the early promise of an oceanic navy went unfulfilled.

ABOVE: **This picture depicts the Federal frigate *Merrimac* before she was captured and partially burned by advancing Confederate forces in Gosport Navy Yard, in Norfolk. Following her capture she was rebuilt as a turtleback ironclad and renamed *Virginia*.** BELOW: **A Union naval gun crew with a boat howitzer on the deck of the monitor USS *Lehigh*. The monitor's circular turret can be seen in the background. Howitzers such as this were designed to be used both from the deck of a vessel and to be taken ashore when appropriate.**

Captain and the end of sail

Captain Cowper Phipps Coles was first inspired to design turntable mountings for heavy guns following the use of ordnance mounted on rafts during the Russian War.

Coles was well aware that the disadvantage of a broadside battery in a steamship was that only half the armament could be brought to bear, and then only on one side or other of the ship's heading. This restricted ships to fighting broadside-on, as they had always done under sail. He advocated turrets for warships and had invented a working mounting so that the guns could be brought to bear at more or less any bearing. Furthermore it was recognized that the weight of Coles's mountings required them to be mounted on the centreline of warships, unlike swivel guns which had long been mounted along the sides.

Even before the clash between *Monitor* and *Virginia*, the British Admiralty had tried Coles's revolving turrets in *Trusty* in 1861, and in 1862 had ordered a coast defence ship, *Prince Albert*, and converted *Royal Sovereign* – a 120-gun three-decker – for coastal defence, each with no less than four turrets. The success of these ships and news about *Monitor* and *Virginia* led to the design of *Monarch*, the first ocean-going turret ship, armed with four 305mm/12in guns in two turrets.

Inefficient engines with high coal consumption meant that ships like *Monarch* still required sails for long passages. However, the forest of masts and rigging which a sailing ship needed was incompatible with centreline turrets, which required clear arcs of fire to be effective. Coles proposed the use of tripod masts to help solve this problem.

Coles was critical of the design of *Monarch*: she was a high-freeboard ship and he was convinced that a low-freeboard design, such as that of *Monitor*, would give additional protection. After he had won the backing of Parliament, the public and *The Times* newspaper, the Admiralty reluctantly ordered a ship from Lairds at Birkenhead to be built to Coles's specification.

While *Captain* was being built between 1867 and 1870 there was insufficient attention to weight control and consequentially she was 813 tonnes/800 tons heavier than planned. Edward Reed, the Admiralty's Chief Constructor, was already concerned about the stability of Coles's design which would have a freeboard of just 2.44m/8ft; however, the additional weight reduced this to just 2m/6ft 6in. The metacentric height was very small so that she rolled slowly; at 14 degrees of heel her gunwales were in the water, and at 21 degrees she was unsafe.

Captain was the first ship of her size to have twin screws, another of Coles's ideas, but she was also given a large sail plan of some 3,715sq m/40,000sq ft. Two revolving centre-line turrets, with twin 305mm/12in, 25.5-tonne/25-ton, muzzle-loading rifled guns firing 270kg/600lb shells, were mounted on the main deck. The stern, midships and forecastles were linked by a flying deck, and restricted the angles of fire or "A" arcs of the guns. The three strongly built masts with tripod supports instead of traditional standing rigging were fitted.

On trials *Captain* appeared to confound her critics; she manoeuvred well under power and was a steady gun platform.

LEFT: **Despite *Captain*'s high sides and continuous upper deck, the men in white uniforms show how low in the ship the guns were mounted. It is evident from the photograph that *Captain* was a low freeboard barbette ship with a dangerously heavy top hamper, which would eventually prove fatal.**
ABOVE: **A close-up of one of *Captain*'s massive turrets shows that the deck above is only a flying bridge. This arrangement kept the rigging clear of the arcs of fire.**

However, the results of heeling experiments in the summer of 1870 were not made known to the Admiralty or to the ship's crew before she sailed to join the Channel Squadron. Onboard was Coles, in the capacity of an observer, and among the midshipmen was the son of Sir Hugh Childers, First Lord of the Admiralty, who had backed Coles against the advice of his own Board of Admiralty.

West of Cape Finisterre Admiral Sir Alexander Milne, Commander-in-Chief of the Mediterranean fleet, had witnessed gunnery practice onboard *Captain*, and as the wind freshened he returned to his flagship, *Lord Warden*. Shortly after midnight on September 7, a strong gust of wind blew out many sails throughout the fleet. *Captain,* however, was knocked over and capsized, sinking quickly, with the loss of 481 of her 499 crew. Ironically, had she been a less strongly built ship the masts might have broken away and saved her.

In the inquiry which followed, blame was shared between the Admiralty, Coles himself and the builder. However, following the disaster no more broadside or central battery ships were laid down, and shortly afterwards the Royal Navy began to reduce the rig of its capital ships, the loss of *Captain* marking the beginning of the end of sail in the Royal Navy.

ABOVE: **A view of *Captain* under construction when her designers and builders lost control of her weight. The photograph shows just how little freeboard she had.** BELOW: ***Captain*'s first voyage was a success and, although this fanciful picture shows her in a storm, with water spilled across her decks, she caused no concern for her stability. She was so strongly built that instead of her sails blowing out or her masts going overboard, the freshening wind caused her to capsize.**

The Battle of Lissa

The Battle of Lissa in the Adriatic in 1866 was the first fleet engagement involving ironclad ships. Even a tactical victory for the Austrians could not save the war for them, but when the gunnery of the day proved ineffective against armour, other navies drew the wrong lessons and ramming was given a bogus tactical status for the rest of the century.

Italy was allied with Prussia, which was fighting Austria for dominance of the German states in the Austro-Prussian or Seven Weeks War. After Prussia had defeated Austria on land, Italy, wanting to gain Italian-speaking provinces from Austria, attempted to use its navy to make territorial gains, and bombarded the island of Lissa or Vis in the eastern Adriatic. The Italian fleet, commanded by Admiral Carlo Persano, included the broadside ironclads: *Regina Maria; Pia San Martino; Castelfidardo; Ancona; Re d'Italia; Re di Portogallo; Principe di Carignano; Terribile;* and *Formidabile;* the turret ram *Affondatore;* and the coast defence ships *Palestro* and *Varese,* This fleet then commenced an assault on the island of Lissa.

The Austrian Admiral Wilhelm von Tegetthoff guarded the Adriatic cities of Pola and Trieste until he became convinced that the island of Lissa was the Italians' main effort, whereupon he immediately set sail for the island. His fleet consisted of the 90-gun ship of the line *Kaiser,* and the broadside ironclads: *Erzherzog Ferdinand Max; Habsburg; Kaiser Max; Prinz Eugen; Juan de Austria; Drache;* and *Salamander.*

As Persano prepared to land on July 20, after two days of bombardment, Tegetthoff appeared out of the fog from the north-west. His fleet was formed into a wedge with the elderly

TOP: **During the Battle of Lissa, the Italian ship *Re d'Italia* was damaged astern and rammed while lying stopped in the water. Her loss gave false authority to the concept of the ram.** ABOVE: **Flagship of the Austrian fleet, the wooden wall *Kaiser* led Tegetthoff's ironclads into battle. It was also damaged in the ramming of *Re D'Italia* and had to be repaired in Malta. Nevertheless, the Battle of Lissa seemed to prove that even a traditional wooden wall could be successfully used as a ram – a false deduction which still deluded naval architects and naval officers for much of the rest of the century.**

Kaiser in the centre of an arrowhead formation of seven ironclads, followed by a second wedge of wooden warships and a convoy of troops.

Although some of Persano's ironclads were absent, he was still numerically superior but his forces were divided and unprepared. Furthermore, he was caught in the middle of landing troops with boats in the water. Persano divided his strength by distributing his ironclads into mixed squadrons with older wooden and sailing ships, and decided, apparently at a late moment, to command his fleet from the *Affondatore.* Forming a hurried line of battle, he is alleged to have said disparagingly of the Austrians, "Here come the fishermen".

Battle commenced at 10.30, when Tegetthoff, still in wedge formation, increased speed and broke the Italian line, rather like Nelson at Trafalgar, ordering his ironclads to turn to port and to sink the enemy centre with their rams. The leading Austrian ironclads then turned to port to attack the Italian centre. In the fierce close-quarters mêlée which ensued, wreathed in smoke from the guns and funnels, Tegetthoff was able to concentrate his seven ironclads against four Italian ironclads. There were several attempts at ramming in which *Ferdinand Max* and *Palestro* succeeded in ramming each other, and Persano in *Affondatore* twice missed hitting *Kaiser*. Then, when *Re d'Italia*'s stern was damaged and she lay stopped in the water, Tegetthoff rammed her at about 11 knots and she sank in a few minutes. Even *Kaiser* somehow managed to damage her bows and had to be sent to the Royal Navy base at Malta for repairs.

Shortly after noon, following two hours of manoeuvring, the Austrian ships were north of Lissa and the Italians to the west; Lissa had been saved. Gunfire continued until mid-afternoon, and at about 14.30 *Palestro* exploded following a fire which had been started during the morning's action. The Italians, now short of coal, retired to Ancona.

The deciding factor in this battle was that the Austrians were better led and better trained, overcoming the Italians' superiority in numbers and quality of ships; however, this was to be overlooked by commentators at the time. Despite the fury of the fight, few ships suffered significant damage and most attempts at ramming had been unsuccessful. However, the Battle of Lissa influenced ship design for the rest of the century, leading to some ships being specifically designed for ramming, even after improvements in gunnery and the development of the torpedo made such tactics suicidal.

The ram has enjoyed a modern reincarnation as the streamlined bulbous bow of merchant ships and in "chin sonars" for frigates, but there is no evidence that it aided ship performance in the 19th century, although architects may have unconsciously discovered how to streamline their designs.

ABOVE: **The Italian coast defence ship *Palestro* and the German battleship *Erzherzog Ferdinand Max* rammed each other during the course of the Battle of Lissa in 1866.** BELOW: **Austria's toehold on the Adriatic included the ancient city-port of Venice and this made her a sea power. The Austrian admiral Wilhelm von Tegetthoff fought in the North Sea as well as at the Battle of Lissa. The Austro-Hungarian navy had global aspirations which included deployments beyond the Mediterranean to the West Indies during the Spanish American War and to China.** BOTTOM: **Late in the deployment and immediately before the battle, the Italian Admiral Carlo Persano transferred his flag to *Affondatore* and lost control of his fleet.**

The Battle of Tsushima

The imperial rivalry between Russia and Japan over control of Manchuria and Korea brought about one of the most decisive battles of naval history. Japan had defeated China in a war in 1894–5, but had been denied her conquests, particularly of Port Arthur on the Liaotung Peninsula, by the international community. In 1896 Russia made a treaty with China which included the right to extend the Trans-Siberian railway across Manchuria to the Russian port of Vladivostok, and two years later gained a lease over Port Arthur. Japan rapidly expanded its army, whilst the railway, which was completed in 1904, enabled Russia to begin a slow build-up of its forces in the Far East. However, when Russia reneged on an agreement to withdraw troops from Manchuria, Japan launched a surprise attack and bombarded Port Arthur and the Russian ships there. The Japanese army overran Korea and the Russian army fell back; Port Arthur was besieged and surrendered on January 2, 1905.

Meanwhile the Russian Baltic Fleet, renamed the Second Pacific Squadron, was despatched from Europe under the command of Admiral Rozhdestvenski. This might have been a fine demonstration of the use of sea power, but the logistic difficulties facing Rozhdestvenski were enormous. Britain, allied with Japan, would not sell coal or grant harbour facilities to the Russians. France, however, granted access to its colonial ports and Germany chartered-out a fleet of 60 colliers of the Hamburg-Amerika Line. Nevertheless, the Russian ships designed either for a 29,000km/18,000-mile voyage nor for tropical conditions, and Russian morale, as well as equipment, seemed to have broken down. A Third Pacific Squadron, composed of weak and elderly ships, transited the Suez Canal to join Rozhdestvenski at Madagascar, where he was delayed while fresh contracts were being drawn up for the supply of coal.

TOP: **The Battle of the Yalu River on August 10, 1904, preceding the Battle of Tsushima. Here the Japanese ships in traditional line-ahead fire the opening shots of the engagement.** ABOVE: **The Japanese fleet under manoeuvre. Every calibre of weapon was fitted in the pre-Dreadnoughts, including machine-guns for anti-torpedo boat defence. These pictures show once more how coal-burning gave away the position of pre-Dreadnought and Dreadnought era battleships. Coal also limited the endurance, measured in speed and range, of coal-powered steamships.**

Kamranh Bay in French Indo-China was the last port before the motley Russian fleet crossed the South China Sea; British-owned Singapore and Hong Kong were, of course, denied to Rozhdestvenski.

There were two routes from Kamranh to Vladivostok. East about the Japanese home islands would require Rozhdestvenski to coal at sea while exposed and open to Japanese attack. The direct route lay west of Japan and led via Tsushima Strait into the Sea of Japan. Steaming slowly to conserve fuel and keep his fleet together, he entered the strait on the night of May 26/27, where the Japanese fleet, commanded by Admiral Togo, was waiting.

Togo was one of several Japanese officers who had been trained by the Royal Navy and he had studied in England from 1871–8. As captain of the cruiser *Naniwa* he had sunk a Chinese troopship en route for Korea, thus precipitating the Sino-Japanese war. His Nelson-like order before the Battle of Tsushima was "The fate of the Empire rests upon this one battle; let every man do his utmost."

Togo's cruisers spotted the Russians heading north-east and reported this by radio. By mid-morning Rozhdestvenski was being followed by two Japanese divisions and Togo while the main battle fleet was approaching from the north. Rozhdestvenski attempted to form a line of battle as ships appeared from the mist and vanished again, but missed signals and poor seamanship threw his ships into confusion.

When the mist cleared in the early afternoon, Togo's concentrated, disciplined and faster fleet was north-east of Rozhdestvenski and on an opposite course. Using his speed, Togo crossed the Russian fleet, which was now in two columns, led his fleet in a 180-degree turn and steadied on a parallel course on the Russians' port side. Later he again crossed the Russians' line of advance, though by now they were in disarray.

The Russians fought bravely but the battle was soon decided. Rozhdestvenski's flagship was one of four Russian battleships destroyed by the concentrated fire of Togo's ships, and with the loss of any kind of central command the battle

TOP: **The Russian *Osliabia*, a Peresviet class battleship, sunk at the Battle of Tsushima in May 1905. Togo's victory over Rozhdestvenski's fleet gave Japan victory in the war.** ABOVE LEFT: **The Russian battleship *Tsessarevitch* photographed in Port Arthur in 1904 where she was blockaded. Her funnels show damage received during the Battle of the Yalu River. The Russians fought bravely in all their engagements, but they were overwhelmed by numbers or by superior logistics.** ABOVE: **A Japanese print showing the destruction of the Russian flagship. Victory marked the ascendancy of the Imperial Japanese Navy and Togo was hailed as the new Nelson.**

became a mêlée and then a massacre. Of the Russian fleet of 45 ships, only two destroyers and the light cruiser *Almaz* reached Vladivostok, and six others reached neutral ports. The rest were sunk, beached, or surrendered.

The battle gave victory to the Japanese in the war, and the annihilation of the Russian fleet altered the balance of power in Europe. Royal Navy officers witnessed the battle from Japanese ships and noted the effectiveness of heavy guns at long range.

The Great White Fleet

The voyage of the Great White Fleet in 1907–9, despatched round the world by the American President Theodore Roosevelt, marked the coming of age of the United States Navy (USN) following a period of revival. The voyage also marked the beginning of the "American" century, presaging the leading role which the USN would take in the 20th century. However despite newspaper acclaim and public pride in the USA, the fleet was obsolescent and to naval planners the voyage revealed strategic weaknesses.

Roosevelt was a navalist who had been influenced by, and then in turn influenced, the American naval strategist Alfred Mahan. As a young man Roosevelt had written *The Naval War of 1812*, which praised the performance of the USN in that war somewhat uncritically, and he had also contributed to Laird Clowes's seven-volume history of the Royal Navy. When Roosevelt became president of the USA, after a period of naval expansion which he himself had helped to stimulate, Japan was beginning to be seen as more of a threat than Britain.

In the summer of 1907 Roosevelt approved a proposal that the American battle fleet should make a demonstration by deploying from the Atlantic to the Pacific coast of the USA. The USN had been considering sending a fleet on a deployment into the Pacific for some time, though quite when Roosevelt agreed that this should become a circumnavigation is not clear. Roosevelt probably only came gradually upon the idea that

such a move would act as a deterrent to the Japanese, impress the American taxpayer, and garner support for more battleships. The long deployment round South America and through the Magellan Straits would also help show the need for the Panama Canal.

ABOVE: **American battleships at Port Said, Egypt. The voyage of the Great White Fleet relied upon a fleet of hired British colliers and upon British-controlled facilities like the Suez Canal.** BELOW: *Connecticut* **leads battleships of the US Atlantic Fleet in 1907. The paint scheme was responsible for the name "white fleet", the supply of coal restricted its operations and smoke gave away its position.**

ABOVE: **Life onboard – a scene which must have been familiar throughout all fleets over many years; peeling vegetables. By the age of steam, however, scurvy was almost unknown.** ABOVE RIGHT: **Rear Admiral C. M. Thomas, USN, onboard *Minnesota*, 1907. The admiral's use of a handheld signal book is another scene which would have been familiar in the age of sail.** RIGHT: **Fourth of July festivities onboard the battleship *Connecticut* in 1908 during the Great White Fleet's historic circumnavigation.**

The battleships were accompanied by several auxiliary ships and, on the first part of their voyage, by a flotilla of early destroyers. The 14-month-long voyage by 14,000 sailors covered some 22,500km/43,000 miles and made 20 landfalls on six continents. They were led initially by Rear Admiral "Fighting Bob" Evans who had made his career in the Spanish-American War.

Significantly, the fleet's first visit was to the British island of Trinidad in the West Indies for coal, and then, on the first leg of its voyage, to Rio de Janeiro, Chile, Peru, Mexico, and on to San Francisco, where *Alabama* and *Maine* were replaced by *Nebraska* and *Wisconsin*. The fleet then visited Hawaii, Auckland, Sydney and Melbourne. The celebrations when the Great White Fleet arrived in Australia in 1908 were only surpassed by those which had been held for the federation of Australia. Over 80,000 people stood on South Head to watch the fleet enter Sydney Harbour and crowds, parties, speeches and parades greeted the Americans. This did not stop American officers from using the opportunity to draw up plans to invade or capture these ports in the event of war with the British Empire.

The fleet then steamed on to Yokohama, Manila, Colombo and Suez, where it arrived on January 3, 1909. The voyage had become something of a race to be home before Roosevelt's successor was sworn in as the new president, and not even an earthquake in Sicily could delay the fleet very much; they were back in Hampton Roads, Virginia, on February 22, 1909.

The voyage of the Great White Fleet may have served its purpose politically, but before they had even set out, every ship had been rendered obsolescent by the launch of the British all-big-gun battleship *Dreadnought*. Just as significantly, the

fleet had found that there were few American bases to support it, and instead the ships had had to rely upon another fleet, of some 50 chartered colliers. Good Welsh or Appalachian coal was unobtainable and the colliers often turned up late with very inferior coal. Worse, the colliers were nearly all British. The lesson was clear; impressive as the Great White Fleet was, the USN would have to (and did) develop its own logistical train.

Within only a few months of returning to the USA the battleships of the Great White Fleet were painted grey and their pole masts were replaced by lattice masts.

The 18 new battleships of the Great White Fleet

Alabama	Kearsarge	Missouri	Vermont
Connecticut	Kentucky	Nebraska	Virginia
Georgia	Louisiana	New Jersey	Wisconsin
Illinois	Maine	Ohio	
Kansas	Minnesota	Rhode Island	

Dreadnoughts and Beyond

While the modern battleship is indelibly linked with Jacky Fisher and his Dreadnought, three other men stand out as having strongly influenced the development of the big gun and the design of the Dreadnought.

At the beginning of the 20th century the Italian naval architect and engineer Vittorio Cuniberti had drawn up plans for a ship with a single calibre of big guns, but the project was regarded as too ambitious for the Italian navy. In 1902 he was given permission to publish an article in *Jane's Fighting Ships*, then a newly established publication. The article was entitled: "An Ideal Battleship for the British Fleet", and his ideas were for "a moderate-sized, very swift vessel with the greatest possible unified armament".

By 1904 navies around the world were about to analyze the Battle of Tsushima and its implications for warship design. At this time guns were laid by eye, so the direction officer needed to see the fall of shot in order to estimate the range adjustment. Cuniberti and others appreciated that as guns of all calibre improved, and could be fired to the limits of visual observation, it was increasingly difficult to distinguish the fall of one shot and thus make the appropriate corrections.

At the same time, in the Royal Navy, Percy Scott was improving the accuracy of gun laying. He had been training commander at the gunnery school, HMS *Excellent*, in Portsmouth, 1890–3; a member of the Ordnance Committee,

ABOVE: **In 1909, *Neptune* was the fastest British battleship to date, and displays the staggered midship turrets favoured by the British.** BELOW: **Fisher's greatest brainchild, *Dreadnought*, was a new type of warship that made all preceding battleships obsolescent, and from which the type took its name.**

1893–6; captain of HMS *Excellent* in 1904; and Inspector of Target Practice in 1908. Scott was a prolific inventor who devised a loading tray to teach faster loading, a "dotter" designed to help his gun layers record accurate bearings, and introduced director firing from a centralized position in the ship. The gunnery technology of the day was capable of firing a shell 16km/10 miles, and Scott helped the Royal Navy to hit targets at these ranges more accurately.

William Sims, a Canadian by birth, joined the USN and between regular appointments was a naval attaché in Europe. Sims reported on new ship designs and improvements in gunnery and wrote directly to President Theodore Roosevelt criticizing the efficiency of the USN. He supported Roosevelt in arguing for the USN adopting an all-big-gun Dreadnought fleet.

Jacky Fisher's unique skill was, therefore, to recognize both the value of advances in naval technology, and to combine them with a knowledge of tactics and an unstoppable drive to carry through reform and development.

As a result of the annihilation of the Russian fleet by the Japanese at the Battle of Tsushima in 1905, the balance of power in Europe was altered. This coincided with the resurgence of the USN and the rise of the German navy. Germany had imperial ambitions, and although its fleet was only intended for a limited purpose, German naval armament was perceived as a threat by Britain, then the greatest naval power in the world. A deadly arms race started across the North Sea, which was a symptom, if not the cause, of World War I. In the event the German warships outside the North Sea were quickly rounded up, and although the Germans adopted tactics intended to defeat the Royal Navy by attrition, they never succeeded.

Der Tag, the day when the two fleets would meet in decisive battle, occurred at Jutland in 1916. Although the Germans won materially, tactically, and in terms of propaganda, it was a disappointment to both sides. The Germans realized too late that submarine warfare was the only way that they could have won the war at sea.

The inter-war years saw the battleship increasingly threatened by two weapons: the submarine and the aeroplane. As these increased in numbers and effectiveness, the battleship could only hold sway up to the start of World War II. Throughout the war, there were sporadic clashes between British and Italian, British and German, and American and Japanese capital ships. However, tactics and operations involving aircraft evolved so rapidly that by 1942 the aircraft carrier, rather than the battleship, was regarded as the new capital ship of the fleet. The British attack on the Italian fleet at Taranto harbour and the crucial damage to *Bismark's* steering gear, which enabled the pursuing surface ships to catch her, were both delivered by airborne torpedo. The attack on Pearl Harbor, which finally brought America into the war, was made by Japanese carrier-borne aircraft, and the pacific theatre was dominated by carrier battles such as those at the Coral Sea, Midway, and the Philippine Sea. By the end of the war battleships were not replaced, although a few lingered on in active service with the USN to operate in a coastal bombardment role.

Where are they now?

A number of examples of battleships from the early phase of their development are still in existence today.

Warrior, the first broadside ironclad, is the only surviving example of the 45 iron hulls built by the Royal Navy between 1861 and 1877. She was obsolete within a decade of being built and placed in reserve. After her masts and guns were stripped, *Warrior* became a depot ship in Portsmouth, attached to the experimental and torpedo training school, and used to supply steam and electricity. She was sold in 1924 and became an oil fuel hulk at Pembroke Dock, Wales. Over the next 50 years some 5,000 ships refuelled alongside her. In 1979 *Warrior* was sold to a trust with a vision of restoring her. This they did at Grays Shipyard in Hartlepool, and she is now on display as a museum ship in Portsmouth, England.

The 1862 *Monitor*, the first of her type, foundered in rough water off Cape Hatteras while under tow by the USS *Rhodes Island*. Her wreck remained lost until it was rediscovered in 1974 – 25.75km/16 miles south-southeast of the Cape, lying upside-down on a relatively sandy bottom at a depth of 73.2m/240ft. Her port side armour belt is exposed at just over 0.3m/1ft above the bottom at the bow, but increasing towards the stern where it is 2.74m/9ft above the sea floor. The starboard armour belt is largely buried in the sandy sediment. The wreck site is now protected as part of the Monitor National Marine Sanctuary and numerous artefacts, including the turret and Dahlgren guns, have been recovered and are on display at the Mariner's Museum, Norfolk, Virginia, USA.

ABOVE: **Lovingly preserved and restored, *Warrior* is now open to the public as a museum ship in Portsmouth, England, a memorial to the ships of her day and the strength of her build.** ABOVE **USS *Monitor* and CSS *Virginia* slug it out to little effect. The submerged wreck of the *Monitor* is currently undergoing detailed examination and a significant number of artefacts have been lifted from the protected site for preservation and public display.**

The *Huascar*, a turret ship built in 1865 for the Peruvian navy, survives in Talcahuano, Chile, and was opened as a museum ship in 1952. The 1868 French-built ironclad ram ship *Schorpioen* of the Royal Netherlands Navy, one of four ships of her class, was restored over a period of seven years in Middleburg by a private foundation, and completed in 1990. In 1998, she was purchased by the Dutch Navy and can now be seen at the Royal Netherlands Navy Museum at Den Helder.

Cerberus, an 1870s British monitor, lies as a deteriorating wreck off the coast of southern Australia where she had first served in Her Majesty's Victoria (state) Navy, and then in the fledgling Australian Navy as a port guard and munitions ship in 1901. In 1926, her hull was purchased by the city of Sandringham and sunk as a breakwater for the Black Rock Yacht Club. Two other monitors also survive – the coastal monitor *Solve*, with her fixed gun, is at Gothenburg, Sweden,

and *M33*, a small bombardment monitor which saw much service in World War I, is in Portsmouth, England.

Built for the Royal Netherlands Navy by Robert Napier and Sons, Glasgow, Scotland in 1868, the turret-ram *Buffel* was one of a pair of ships to incorporate the latest contemporary design features: twin guns in a covered revolving turret, armoured sides, and a ram bow based on the somewhat dubious conclusions drawn from the Battle of Lissa. Primarily designed as a coastal-defence ship to operate within easy reach of coal supplies, she was reduced to a barracks ship in 1896. Having miraculously survived World War II laid up in Amsterdam, she was beautifully restored to her original state between 1974 and 1979, and is now at the Maritime Museum Prins Hendrick in Rotterdam, the Netherlands.

Mikasa, the 1902 pre-Dreadnought flagship of the Japanese navy at the Battle of Tsushima, is now embedded in concrete in Yokosuka, Japan. Preservation of this vessel was cast in some doubt at the end of World War II, when the USSR wanted her to be scrapped but the USA wished to preserve her. A compromise was eventually reached whereby she was stripped of her fittings but not scrapped; however, 15 years later, she was fully restored, largely as a result of help offered by US Admiral Chester Nimitz.

The 1889 British pre-Dreadnought *Hood* lies upside down outside the breakwater at Portland, England, where she was sunk as a block ship in 1914. Today she is known as "Old hole in the wall" and is a popular dive site. The wreck of the 1893 USS *Massachusetts* is an underwater archaeological preserve off Pensacola, Florida.

ABOVE: **Now a rather sad and rapidly deteriorating wreck off the coast of South Australia where she was sunk as a breakwater, the British monitor *Cerberus* is seen here in happier days.** BELOW: **HMS *Hood*, not to be confused with her later namesake and victim of the *Bismark*, now lies upside down outside the breakwater at Portland, England, where she is a popular dive site.**

Pre-Dreadnoughts

The pre-Dreadnought battleships were a bewildering variety of vessels. Once the propeller had been married to steam propulsion, the choice for naval architects was between broadside and turreted guns. The first turrets were fitted on to small ships. Because of their weight, they could not be mounted in larger ships until steam engines became more reliable and the top hamper represented by masts and sails could be done away with. As armour temporarily outstripped the effectiveness of guns, the ram was thought to be the weapon of choice at sea and survived a remarkably long time until the torpedo and long range guns became available. Once all the elements of the modern battleship were present, the final problem to solve was that of hitting the target at long range. Before the use of radar, the only way of spotting the fall of shot was by eye and for accurate range-finding a single large calibre with all the guns slaved to a single fire control was necessary. Only when all these design problems had been resolved and the technology developed could the modern Dreadnought battleship come into being.

LEFT: *Implacable* sweeping majestically out of Malta, whose harbours were the proud base of the Royal Navy for more than a century and a half.

Gloire

In the Russian War 1854–6 Britain and France had formed an unlikely alliance against Russia, and during the war both navies had constructed armoured floating batteries, and used these to effect in the Black Sea against shore targets. Once the war was over France continued to develop the concept of an ironclad ship, primarily as a means of opposing her ancient enemy, Britain, and between 1858 and 1861 ordered no less than 16 broadside ironclads.

The first three, designed by Dupuy de Lôme, were Gloire and Invincible, laid down at Toulon in 1858, and, a few months later, Normandie at Cherbourg.

They were wooden-hulled and clad in wrought-iron armour. The hulls were 0.6m/2ft thick and covered by an armoured belt over 100mm/4in thick which extended from stem to stern and to 1.83m/6ft below the waterline, and there was a thinner layer of plating under the wooden upper deck. In the style of the screw ships that Gloire would replace, she was pierced for 38 guns on the main deck, although she never seems to have carried so many, an arrangement carried over from the days of sail. The armament differed throughout the class and with time. In Gloire, the original guns themselves were 160mm/6.4in rifled muzzle-loaders, although in an age when the technology of

ABOVE: **Despite having been recent allies in the Russian War, the French began building new ships in the late 1850s which would challenge the Royal Navy. The first of these was** *Gloire*, **a wooden-hulled ironclad ship incorporating the lessons which had been learned about the effect of modern guns. The use of wood limited the length of the hull.**

guns was also evolving rapidly, these were successively replaced by breech-loaders of different sizes. There were also four Paixhans shell guns on the upper deck.

Originally barquentine-rigged, the sail area was doubled to 2,500sq m/27,000sq ft when these ships were converted to ship-rig, but they were no more successful, despite French insistence upon building four of the class. Normandie and Invincible were built of poor timber that soon rotted and both were hulked up in 1871–2. Nevertheless, Normandie was the first armoured ship to cross the Atlantic, when she was sent to Mexico in 1862–3 in furtherance of Napoleon III's ambitions to found an empire there, but she returned with a centuries-old problem, an outbreak of yellow fever. Gloire lasted until 1879.

Ships of the Gloire class rolled badly and were not otherwise successful ships, nevertheless to France must go the honour of building the first armoured battleship.

When intelligence reached Britain of these new ships, there was an immediate response in the building of *Warrior*, a ship in every respect superior to *Gloire*. *Warrior* was not only larger by nearly 4,065 tonnes/4,000 tons, but faster and more heavily armed. Symbolically, the second of these ships was named *Black Prince*. It is surprising, therefore, that France, having introduced the first innovation, continued with her programme to build ships that were so much weaker than the British vessels.

Innovation nevertheless continued, and on the same day that *Gloire* was ordered, so was the iron-hulled *Couronne*. Though launched and completed after the *Warrior*, due to alteration to her plans during building, *Couronne* was another first for France: the world's first iron-hulled armoured battleship. Though similar in appearance to *Gloire*, her armour was unusual, consisting of a sandwich of teak, an iron lattice-work and more teak clad in iron plating. The upper deck armour was thicker, but did not cover the engine room spaces. There was no compartmentation, and in her last manifestation she was armed with eight 240mm/9.4in and four 190mm/7.6in guns on the main gundeck and two 120mm/4.7in and 12 1-pounder guns on the upper deck.

The French programme seemed unstoppable, and included two two-decker ironclads, also designed by Dupuy de Lôme and the only ships of their type ever built, *Magenta* and *Solferino*. They were also the first ships to have a spur ram, which projected 19.5m/64ft and was covered by a 14,225kg/14 ton steel cone, though their wide turning circle rendered them tactically unsuitable for ramming. The armament varied throughout their careers, and eventually the lower gundeck was removed. In another novelty, they carried two howitzers on the upper deck, capable of raining fire on an enemy ship.

Seemingly content with the *Gloire* design, a class of ten ships were all laid down in 1861, and all were wooden-hulled except the last, *Heroine*. Although the design had started a

TOP: **The British response to *Gloire* was immediate. *Warrior* was an iron-built, armoured ship, twice as big, twice as fast and twice as powerful as the French *Gloire* and her sisters.** ABOVE: **With the launch of *Warrior*, and *Black Prince* – a name surely chosen to send a message to the French – Britain and the Royal Navy announced their intention to maintain supremacy at sea.**

revolution and precipitated a naval arms race with Britain, many of these were still afloat in the 1890s when developments in gunnery made them obsolete, so strongly built were the hulls.

Gloire class

Class: *Gloire, Invincible, Normandie.*
  Launched 1859–61
Dimensions: Length (at waterline) –
  77.9m/255ft 6in
  Beam – 17m/55ft 9in
  Draught – 8.5m/27ft 10in
Displacement: 5,720 tonnes/5,630 tons
Armament: Main – 36 x 160mm/6.4in
  RML guns
Machinery: 1-shaft HRCR, 8 oval boilers,
  1,864kW/2,500ihp
Performance: 13 knots
Complement: 570 men

Warrior

By the mid-1850s, and the end of the Russian War, Britain was the world's foremost industrial nation and the Royal Navy had an overwhelming superiority in three-decker screw ships. It was policy to observe other nations' innovations and then use Britain's industrial and shipbuilding might to maintain the Royal Navy's supremacy. News from France of *Gloire* called this policy into action and in 1859 two ships were ordered, *Warrior* and *Black Prince*, designed by chief constructor Isaac Watts and engineer John Scott Russell. Unlike *Gloire* they were constructed of iron frames (in which the Victorian engineers excelled), which allowed a longer and stronger ship.

They were initially classed as frigates, because of their single main gundeck, and when completed they were the world's most powerful warships. Their strength lay not only in a broadside, on build, of ten 110-pounder, 26 68-pounder and four 70-pounder guns, but a complement of over 700 seamen and marines with field guns, muskets and cutlasses for warfare ashore.

Their high length-to-beam ratio (6.5:1) and fine lines forward and aft made them fast ships, though at slow speed they were not very handy. Ship-rigged, *Warrior* had a lifting screw and logged 13 knots under sail, while *Black Prince*, with a fixed screw, managed only 11 knots, but under combined sail and steam both ships could reach 17 knots. With taller funnels for increased draught to the boilers *Warrior* exceeded 14 knots under steam alone. The armour belt over the midships sections was 64.9m/213ft long and 6.7m/22ft deep and consisted of iron plates 4.6m/15ft by 0.9m/3ft and weighing 4,060kg/4 tons each which slotted together by tongue and groove. Other novel features included steam-driven capstans and watertight, armoured bulkheads fore and aft, and double bottoms that were compartmented. They were quite simply the biggest, the fastest and best armed and armoured ships in the world.

However, the British Admiralty was more concerned about the increased costs than the threat from France, so while continuing to build older-style wooden ships, the follow-on ships, *Defence* and *Resistance*, were smaller by about one third (6,100 tonnes/6,000 tons rather than 9,140 tonnes/9,000 tons). Then, when the French announced a programme to construct 30 seagoing ironclads, work on wooden line-of-battle ships halted. Instead two more ships of the Defence class, *Hector* and *Valiant*, were laid down, as were four *Warrior*-sized ships, the four-masted *Achilles*, and the magnificent five-

BELOW: **Warrior was so strongly built that she has survived until today and can now be seen as a beautifully restored museum ship in Portsmouth, where, with her towering masts, she is one of the first and most memorable sights to greet the visitor to the several naval museums there.**

LEFT: **An interior view of the preserved and restored *Warrior*. Modern armour and heavy guns were not all – on the bulkhead behind the gun is a rack of small arms, intended for use when *Warrior* landed her sailors and marines for power projection ashore.** BELOW: ***Warrior* shortly after she arrived at Hartlepool for restoration by the Warrior Preservation Trust.** BOTTOM: ***Warrior* in dry dock sometime in the 1870s. Her figurehead has been beautifully restored.**

masted 10,770 tonne/10,600 ton *Minotaur, Agincourt* and *Northumberland*. Also five (originally eight) 90-gun two-deckers, *Prince Consort, Caledonia, Ocean, Royal Oak* and *Royal Alfred*, were converted on the slips to wooden broadside ironclads and some purpose-built wooden broadside ironclads, including *Lord Clyde* and *Lord Warden*, were built to use up existing timber stocks. All of these ships were larger, faster and better armed than the Provence class, to a degree that ought to have deterred the French. By 1867, the Royal Navy had completed 19 broadside battery ships, easily outbuilding the French whose challenge collapsed for want of finance, industrial capacity and adequate designs.

The only area in which the British ironclads were possibly inferior was that they were armed with muzzle-loading guns. When *Warrior* was completed in 1861, Armstrong rifled breech-loaders were widely fitted throughout the fleet, but a series of accidents from flaws in the steel barrels and in the breech mechanisms caused these to be abandoned. For the next few years, the British Navy reverted to using a muzzle-loading rifled gun until by the 1880s the technology was sufficiently advanced, in other navies, for a reliable breech-loading gun to replace smooth bore guns.

These ships spanned an age of change. *Achilles* as completed in 1864 was the only British warship with four masts and had the largest sail area of any British warship. *Lord Warden* (1867) at 7,968 tonnes/7,842 tons was the heaviest wooden ship ever built and *Minotaur* the first ship to carry a searchlight. The *Hector* as a tender at the Royal Navy's

experimental school, Vernon, was the first ship to be fitted with wireless, in 1900. Many of these ships also had exceptionally long lives: *Minotaur* and *Black Prince* were broken up in 1923, *Achilles* in 1925, *Northumberland* in 1927, *Defence* in 1935, *Valiant* in 1957, and *Agincourt* not until 1960. *Warrior* is still afloat and has been fully restored as a museum ship. She was restored internally and externally at Hartlepool before being towed to her present berth in Portsmouth.

Warrior

Class: *Warrior, Black Prince*.
  Launched 1860–1
Dimensions: Length (at waterline) –
  115.9m/380ft 2in
  Beam – 18m/58ft 4in
  Draught – 7.9m/26ft
Displacement: 9,284 tonnes/9,137 tons
Armament: Main – 4 x 205mm/8in MLR guns
  Secondary – 28 x 180mm/7in MLR
  and 4 x 20pdr BL guns
Machinery: 1-shaft, Penn HSET, 10 rectangular
  boilers, 3,928kW/5,267ihp
Performance: 14 knots
Complement: 707 men

The first *Monitor*

*M*onitor was only one of 17 proposals considered by the Federal government of the USA in 1861, of which three were selected for construction: the conventional broadside-ironclad *New Ironsides*, the armoured ship *Galena*, and the wholly unconventional *Monitor,* which was designed by John Ericsson. Ericsson's ship was an armoured wooden raft, with a lower hull 38m/126ft long and 10.3m/34ft wide, overhung, turtle-fashion, by a platform 52.5m/172ft long and 12.5m/41ft wide: the overhang protected the sides, propeller and screw from ramming.

The USN had asked for a speed of 8 knots, but *Monitor*'s best speed was only 6 knots. Worse, the freeboard was only 35.5cm/14in, though the largely submerged hull, often awash, was less susceptible to rolling. The hatches, however, could only be opened in the calmest of weather and the hawse pipe in the hull was very near the waterline. The forced-air ventilators were 1.37m/4ft 6in high and the two square funnels were 1.83m/6ft high: even with forced ventilation temperatures inside *Monitor* were intolerable.

Ericsson's original sketch called for 150mm/6in armour on the side and 50mm/2in on the deck, made up of individual 25.4mm/1in plates bolted or riveted together. This, it was

TOP: *Merrimac* was rated by the USN as an auxiliary screw frigate when her burned hulk was captured alongside by the Confederate forces, who rebuilt her as an ironclad. ABOVE: John Ericsson, who was one of a group of Swedes who strongly influenced the USN in the mid-19th century. Ericsson was a prolific inventor who designed the first monitor.

calculated, would have sunk the *Monitor* and the side armour was reduced to 50mm/2in except around the turret where it was 200–230mm/8–9in. A pilothouse on the foredeck was built of 230mm/9in iron blocks.

Ericsson's heavily armoured, shallow-draft iron hull with its low profile had good protection against cannon shot and the unusual construction protected the vital parts from damage by ramming.

LEFT: **The launch of the first monitor. The name was chosen because, according to Gustavus Fox (another Swede), she was going to teach the Confederates – and the British – a lesson.**
BELOW: **In the battle between *Monitor* and *Merrimac* (now renamed *Virginia*) neither ship could really damage the other and when *Monitor* retreated into shallow water, *Virginia* could not follow.** BOTTOM: **This diagram shows the saucer-like profile of *Monitor*. Ericsson also devised a novel turret (not shown here) mounted on a spindle.**

The USN would have preferred a low-board ironclad with turrets on the Coles principle of a roller bearing, but Ericsson provided a single turret mounted on a central spindle with a bronze skirt resting on a ring of bronze. The turret was 6.1m/20ft in diameter and 2.74m/9ft high, and the roof was made of a grating of railway lines. The turret held two 280mm/11in Dahlgren smoothbore shell guns, and was powered by steam. The steam mechanism made training the guns jerky and imprecise.

Monitor was unlikely to teach the British Admiralty any lessons but she was well suited for coastal and riverine warfare during the American Civil War.

Built in a few months in the winter of 1861/2 at the Continental Iron Works in Greenpoint, Long Island, *Monitor* left New York after trials on March 6. She experienced heavy weather on her route south, and her exhausted crew reached Hampton Roads two days later. She fought her famous action against the *Merrimac*, the first between two armoured ships, on March 9, 1862. Neither ship could seriously harm the other and a further fight in April, after *Merrimac* had been improved by fitting more armour and now equipped with solid shot, was declined.

Monitor fought in the James River in support of the Army's Peninsular Campaign, before being sent to Washington for improvements that included a telescopic funnel, better ventilation, and davits. However, on December 31, 1862 *Monitor* was returning to operations in the South when she was caught in rough waters off Cape Hatteras and flooded by seawater that drowned her boilers. She foundered and 16 of her crew of 62 were lost.

The wreck of *Monitor* was rediscovered in 1974 and is on display at the Mariners' Museum, Norfolk, Virginia.

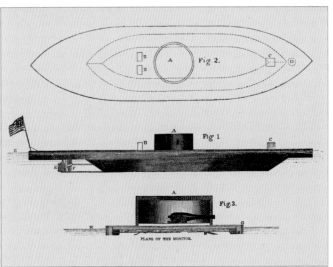

PLANS OF THE MONITOR.

Virginia

After the Federal frigate *Merrimac* was captured alongside and partly burned in Gosport Navy Yard in Norfolk by advancing Confederate forces, she was successfully converted into an ironclad of unusual design. At the same time she was renamed *Virginia*.

Virginia was armed with a mix of guns behind an armoured casemate. This casemate was 51.8m/170ft long sloping inwards and upwards, and covered with layers of plates both horizontally and vertically. She had two significant disadvantages: her engines were not powerful enough for the additional weight of armour so she took a long time to manoeuvre, and she had the draught of a frigate, so that she was unsuited for warfare in estuaries and rivers.

However, on March 8, 1862 she attacked the blockading Federal fleet in Hampton Roads, sank the frigate *Congress* and the sloop *Cumberland*,

and could have turned the tide of the war. The next day when she renewed her attack she found *Monitor* had arrived. Neither ship could harm the other much and *Monitor* escaped into shallower water, where *Virginia* with her deeper draught could not follow.

As Union forces continued to advance, *Virginia* was destroyed by her crew in May 1862.

TOP: **The retreating Federal forces burned *Merrimac* to the waterline, so it was a relatively simple matter to convert her to a turtleback ironclad. News of the conversion inspired the North to build *Monitor*.**

ABOVE: **This turtleback ironclad of unusual design was renamed *Virginia* after conversion. The sloping sides of the armour helped to protect her by letting shot glance off, and she was eventually destroyed by her own crew as the Union forces continued to advance.**

Broadside ironclads

The building of broadside ironclads in the late 1850s and 1860s was stimulated by Anglo-French rivalry and the threat of war in northern and southern Europe.

In order to overmatch the French Gloire class, Britain, in addition to building iron-hulled broadside ships, converted a number of 90-gun wooden ships to ironclads in 1860–4, and other navies followed suit. Denmark, which was faced with the inevitability of war with Prussia over Schleswig-Holstein, converted *Dannebrog*, a 72-gun two-deck sailing ship, in 1863. Russia converted two frigates, *Sevastopol* and *Petropavlovsk*, to ironclads, and perhaps the oldest ship to be converted was the Dutch *De Ruyter*, first built as a 74-gun ship in 1831.

Interest in the Gloire class attracted customers to France, where broadside ironclads and central battery ships were built for foreign customers including Germany. The Italian navy, which was created in 1861 from the navies of Naples, Piedmont-Sardinia, Tuscany, the two Sicilies and the Papal States, bought purpose-built ships from yards abroad, including the French-built *Terrible* and *Formidable* and the Regina Maria Pia class, but the two kings, *Re d'Italia* and *Re di Portogallo*, were bought in the USA. As its industry developed, Italy began to design and build her own ships in yards in Genoa and Leghorn. Austria

responded by using her indigenous shipbuilding capacity at Trieste to build the Drache and Kaiser Max classes.

Spain bought one ironclad broadside from France, *Numancia*, and built another, *Tetuan*, at Ferrol, while the iron-hulled *Vitoria* and former wooden screw frigate *Arapiles* were built or converted on the Thames.

Turkey also ordered new-build ironclads from British yards, *Osmanieh, Mahmudieh, Abdul Aziz* and *Orkanieh*. This started the habit of the Royal Navy using foreign ships being built in British yards as a reserve of ships ready to be taken over in time of crisis.

The broadside ironclad was the end of the evolution of the ship of the line rather than a step in the development of the battleship. The new navies of Japan and Germany missed this phase altogether.

BELOW: **It was difficult to mount turrets in ocean-going ships and so broadside ironclads continued to be built for a number of years, including the 1864 French *Surveillante*.** BOTTOM LEFT: **Marking another stage in the evolution of the battleship, while retaining the broadside layout, *Deutschland*'s armament was almost all confined to an armoured central citadel.** BOTTOM: **While looking like a broadside ironclad, the 1865 Italian *Roma* combined several features including a ram and central battery.**

The monitors

Over 50 monitors were ordered during the American Civil War although many were not completed, and most were sold or broken up within ten years. When a new generation of monitors was built, Amphitrite class (1874), Monterey (1889) and Arkansas class (1899), they took the names of Civil War ships of which they were supposed to be "repairs".

In an attempt to make them seagoing, masts and super-structures were added, and the 3,455-tonne/3,400-ton *Miantonomoh* made a trans-Atlantic voyage, mostly under tow, with the Secretary of the Navy, Gustavus Vasa Fox, on board. Despite Fox's ambition that these monitors would teach the British a lesson, *Miantonomoh* had to use Royal Navy resources in Halifax, St John's, Queenstown, Portsmouth and Gibraltar to accomplish her remarkable journey. During a visit to France, Fox called on Napoleon III and his travels took him to Denmark in July 1866. He also visited St Petersburg in August for a month-long visit – although what the autocratic Tsar Alexander II thought of the representative of an upstart republic named after the king of one of his country's bitterest enemies is not known. Fox's aim was to study European naval

ABOVE: *Cerberus* was built in England to the order of the Australian state of Victoria. Her sides were built up and she was ship-rigged for her oceanic voyage of delivery. The remains of *Cerberus* can still be seen where she was sunk as a breakwater, though she is probably too far gone ever to be restored, and within a few years she will probably be lost forever.

technology, though naturally his ship excited much interest. *Miantonomoh* returned via Sweden, Germany, France, Portugal, Spain and Italy and in May 1867 crossed the Atlantic via a more southerly route and one last call, courtesy of the British, for more coal in the Bahamas, a journey of a staggering 28,587km/ 17,767 miles.

Used effectively in the waterways and rivers, the perceived success of the monitors resulted in them being copied by other nations, including Sweden, Norway and the Netherlands. The Swedes built American-style monitors also designed by Ericsson, who gifted guns built by Dahlgren, and the first ship in 1865 was called *John Ericsson*. Though initially armed with two 380mm/15in guns these were replaced in 1881 with 240mm/9.4in guns. *John Ericsson* had two sister ships, *Thordön*

ABOVE: **In addition to her twin 255mm/10in guns** *Cerberus* **carried a range of lesser guns. Here her crew are demonstrating how those guns would be manned.**
ABOVE RIGHT: **The Swedish monitor** *John Ericsson*. **Despite his work in the United States, Ericsson retained links with his country of birth and both he and fellow-Swede John Dahlgren represented designs and surplus equipment to the Swedish navy.** RIGHT: **Surprisingly the USN was still operating 19th-century-style monitors in World War I. Some even crossed the Atlantic and others were used as submarine depot ships, for which their low freeboard was especially suitable.**

(1866) and *Tirfing* (1867) and a slighter larger sister ship, *Loke* (1871). All had the low freeboards typical of their type and even in the slightest sea, the upper decks were awash.

Even the Royal Navy built some monitors, the oldest surviving being the *Cerberus*, built at Jarrow on the Tyne in 1867–8 and fitted out at Chatham. At Chatham the Admiralty refused to let her fly the White Ensign or even to provide naval victuals and the civil authorities refused to register her as a merchant ship, while her first Captain died of illness. Finally, an officer was sent from Melbourne to bring her to Victoria, Australia. Since her freeboard was only 0.91m/3ft, temporary bulwarks were fitted and she was rigged with masts and sail, which were useless for making headway but they steadied her when she ran into heavy weather. With bunkers for only 122 tonnes/120 tons of coal, she had to rely on frequent coalings, which gave plenty of opportunity for her crew to desert or mutiny, which they did in Portsmouth and Malta, preferring a spell in prison to the risks of the voyage, and the searing heat between decks. It did not help that another new-fangled ship, *Captain*, had capsized in heavy weather with large loss of life only a few weeks before.

However, *Cerberus* was the first steamship to combine a central superstructure with fore and aft gun turrets, and the first armoured warship built for Australia. In dispensing with sail power she preceded the Royal Navy's *Devastation* by three years, and she was the first steamship to pass through the newly completed Suez Canal. Once *Cerberus* reached Port Philip in 1871 she never left and, apart from an American plan to capture Melbourne prepared during the visit of the Great White Fleet, no one ever challenged the guardian of the hull's four 255mm/10in rifled muzzle-loading Armstrong guns. Her remains – she was scuttled as a breakwater off the Black Rock Yacht Club – are the oldest surviving warship to have served in the Royal Australian Navy.

Although the 20th century would witness a revival of the type, the low-freeboard monitor was a dead-end in battleship development. *Devastation*, with a similar layout but three times the size of *Cerberus*, did however set the pattern for future battleships. Amazingly some USN monitors continued to cross the Atlantic without being swamped and were used as submarine tenders in World War I where their low-freeboard was an advantage.

LEFT: **The French cruiser *Dupuy de Lôme* exhibits an extreme form of the ram. The French navy at the end of the 19th century was well known for its odd, even extreme, designs. Possibly naming this ship after one of the better naval architects was an attempt to legitimize the design.**

The rams

In the American Civil War, several ships were attacked by ramming, causing John Ericsson to design into *Monitor* elaborate features to protect her underwater form from ramming. The French were the first to construct a seagoing ram, the wooden-hulled armoured *Taureau* in 1863, which was built with a turtle deck, a large gun in a barbette and a long-spur ram, however she rarely left harbour.

The French were no more successful with the larger *Cerbere* class in 1865. However, the idea of ramming was boosted by the sinking of the *Re d'Italia* during the Battle of Lissa in 1866. Analysts failed to note that the *Re d'Italia* had already suffered rudder damage and was unable to manoeuvre out of the way.

In 1868, the Royal Navy responded with the ironclad ram *Hotspur*, an iron-hulled ship of 4,064 tonnes/4,000 tons whose ram projected 3.05m/10ft, but the low freeboard gave poor seakeeping qualities and she was only used for coastal defence. The much larger *Rupert* of 5,527 tonnes/5,440 tons was built in 1870 but was not much better, though both ships were modernized and survived into the 20th century.

Then in 1871, the British Admiralty's committee on Designs for Ships of War highlighted what it called the importance of ramming. Consequently, the British built the freakish torpedo ram *Polyphemus* in 1878, and the monstrous 6,096-tonne/6,000-ton turret rams *Conqueror* and *Hero* in 1879 and 1884, armed with 305mm/12in breech-loading guns. Naval officers and architects had just about overcome their nervousness when in 1893 *Camperdown* struck *Victoria*, though *Victoria*'s rapid sinking was due to poor inherent stability. Most pre-Dreadnought battleships were built with rams and Jacky Fisher even chose a design for *Dreadnought* that gave the appearance that she had a ram.

Nevertheless, it was a failed tactic: ramming could be effective only against ships that were unable to manoeuvre, and there was at least as much risk of damage to the ramming vessel as there was to the target in the approach under fire and in any collision. Rams may however have acted as bulbous bows and bestowed some streamlining on the pre-Dreadnoughts, and fear of ramming helped to improve damage control and promote the internal subdivision of ships.

BELOW: **A British battleship in dry dock showing her ram. Note also the open hatches of her forward-firing anti-torpedo-boat guns and booms for her anti-torpedo nets.**

Barbettes

The first ironclad warships mounted guns in broadsides just like their sailing ship predecessors. At first during the battleship revolution ships' sides were protected by iron cladding and then individual guns were protected by shields. At the same time the early monitors and some small warships had turrets with roofs after designs by Coles and Ericsson. Smaller ironclad warships continued to be armed with guns in broadsides, but as the size of gun and the thickness of armour increased they were placed in armoured batteries known as casements.

As gun size increased again warships were generally fitted with fewer guns and these had to be sited on the centreline of low-freeboard ships and placed inside barbettes or fixed iron shields inside which the guns rotated on their mountings. The term barbette came to be applied to the open-topped, armoured enclosure used to protect guns on their turntable together with their crews. The guns fired over the top of their barbettes, but when roofs were added to mountings from the mid-1860s onwards, they became known as turrets again, and the name barbette was applied to the internal substructure which extended below deck. However, when it was introduced the barbette was considered an advance in naval

construction as it saved weight when compared to building a larger turret.

For example, the 9,144-tonne/9,000-ton *Devastation* and *Thunderer* of 1869 had muzzle-loading rifled 305mm/12in guns in twin turrets, fore and aft, but *Collingwood* of 1880 was 508 tonnes/ 500 tons larger and mounted her guns in barbettes. The barbettes in *Collingwood* were pear-shaped, 15.24m/50ft long and 13.72m/45ft wide, with an armoured trunk at the rear of the barbette for the ammunition hoist (compare with *Dreadnought* below), and the general layout proved to be the model for the majority of pre-Dreadnought battleships.

In 1868 the French were the first to build a barbette, to a British design, which penetrated the deck with an armoured trunk resting on the well-protected roller path. This enabled the French to build high-sided ships with their main guns well clear of the water but they proved to be vulnerable to gunfire and the ships of the Hoche class were held to be some of the worst French designs, despite many modifications while building. They were so heavy that most of the armour was underwater but they did have comfortable accommodation and were accordingly known as the grand hotels. The French also introduced splinter shields over the mountings to protect

their crews and by the 1890s this was the standard method of mounting heavy guns in battleships.

In Britain the *Royal Sovereign* of 1892 was one of the first designs in which the barbette was extended below deck to afford some protection to the magazine and ammunition hoists. In the *Majestic* of 1895 the barbette revolved with the gun, although the gun still had to return to a fixed angle of elevation and training for loading. The Italian *Re Umberto* of 1893 and British *Caesar* and *Illustrious* of 1895 were the first ships to have guns which could be loaded at any angle.

The design of the barbette required a very large diameter and one of the frequently overlooked but revolutionary aspects of the 1905 *Dreadnought* was her compact turrets with an internal diameter of just 8.23m/27ft.

The earliest ironclads still had wooden mountings with guns on trucks or slides whose recoil was controlled by ropes, but as the guns grew in size so pivoting iron slides and friction and later hydraulic means of restraining the recoil were introduced. The early guns' mountings in their barbettes were trained by hand although steam-powered, hydraulic and eventually electrical systems were later developed. Finally by about 1900 the barbette was no longer a feature of warship design.

LEFT: **The French *Tonnant* (1880) was intended as a coast defence ship to keep the British at bay. Note the barbettes are roofed over to protect the gun's crew from splinters.** ABOVE: **The French persisted in barbette mountings for their guns, as in *Magenta* (1890), though the larger hull enabled their designers to build more seaworthy ships.**

Turret ships

The French are credited with having introduced armoured floating batteries in the Crimea, during the Russian War of 1854–6, in order to attack Russian positions in support of the attack on Kinburn.

It was during the Russian War that British Captain Cowper Coles and the Swede, John Ericsson, made proposals for turret ships. Ericsson, after several years of attempting to interest the Royal Navy in his various inventions, had settled in the USA and there he successfully introduced a design that became known as a monitor. The USA became a prolific builder of monitors, and many other navies took up similar designs. In its simplest form the monitor remained a platform for bombarding the shore, though some of these grew to be quite large. Some subsequent designs such as the coast defence ship had many attributes of the true battleship.

However, real navies needed seagoing vessels capable of standing up to the heaviest ships in any other navy's order of battle. In the late 1850s, Cowper Coles made many proposals for ships fitted with guns mounted in cupolas including an 1859 plan for a ship with ten armoured cupolas. In response, the Royal Navy cautiously tried out an experimental turret in *Trusty* in 1861. The problem was to design a ship capable of crossing oceans, or in the British case the Channel, that could carry sufficient armour and armament to defeat any shallow-water monitor that might be waiting on the other side. Two of Cowper

Coles's designs were the Danish *Rolf Krake* (1863), and the Peruvian *Huascar* (1865), which did indeed cross open waters, but neither could be regarded as successful.

Rolf Krake, also described as an armoured battery ship, entered the Danish navy in 1863. Built by Napier & Sons in Glasgow she was the first Danish ship to be iron-built and carried four 205mm/8in guns in two double turrets mounted on

BELOW: **Showing how alternative designs co-existed, the *Dreadnought* (1875) had her funnels and other top hamper centralized amidships. Here she is cleared for action and her boats are being towed astern.** BOTTOM: **The British *Agamemnon* (1879) had turret mountings and, in an echo of the earlier, failed *Captain* design, these were mounted one deck lower with forecastle and aftercastle and flying bridge to carry the boats, searchlights and so on.**

the centre-line. The turrets rotated on a roller track which also supported their weight (unlike Ericsson's design for the first monitor in which the turret rested and rotated a central spindle). However, the fundamental principle that turrets should be mounted on the centre-line was soon lost as ships grew bigger, and was not rediscovered until the epoch-making *Dreadnought* was built in 1905. *Rolf Krake* took part in the War of Schleswig Holstein in 1854 and although not a decisive influence on the course of the war, she helped to persuade the German emperor that Germany needed to build its own navy.

Huascar was also built in Britain according to a Coles design. She was twice tested in battle, against two unarmoured British cruisers in 1877, and against several Chilean sailing ships and two casemate ships in 1879. *Huascar* was captured by the Chileans and has been maintained as a trophy of war ever since.

The first British turret ship was the *Royal Sovereign*, formerly a three-deck line-of-battle ship, launched in 1849, which was cut down in 1862 and armed with 265mm/10.5in guns in a twin turret and three single turrets. She remained in service for a surprisingly long time as a coast defence ship. The first purpose-built design was the *Prince Albert* in 1866, whose 230mm/9in guns barely qualify her for a mention in this book but which, it is said, remained in commission until 1899 in deference to Queen Victoria's wishes.

The disadvantage with turrets was their weight, the main issue being that as the size of the gun increased, so too did the weight of armour and these large weights could not be carried high in the hull without risk of instability. The result was a number of low-freeboard ships with poor seakeeping qualities.

The problem is clearly demonstrated in the case of the seven battleships of the Royal Sovereign class of 1889–91 and the eighth ship ordered at the same time under the Naval Defence Act, *Hood*. All had similar 340mm/13.5in guns, but in

TOP: **The turret armour-clad *Devastation* at a naval review at Spithead (for the visit of the Shah of Persia) on June 23, 1873, painted by E. Wake Cooke and capturing the power and majesty of the new pre-Dreadnoughts.** ABOVE: **The German *Preussen*, photographed in Malta in 1890, is a turret ship; though even with her sailing rig reduced from the original she still displays many of the characteristics of a former generation of ships.**

the former, they were in barbettes. However, in order to carry the weight of a turret in *Hood*, the guns had to be fitted one deck lower.

The turret was the correct line for development rather than the barbette, but guns in turrets would not become standard until a smaller size of gun was established at 305mm/12in and the effectiveness of armour had also improved. This would allow the turret weight to be reduced, whilst the displacement of the battleship increased significantly.

Coast defence ships

The American Civil War was followed closely in Europe, and particularly in the Royal Navy, where a 121-gun ship of the line, *Royal Sovereign,* was turned into a coast defence battleship. The conversion in 1862 was not as extreme as that of the *Virginia,* because the *Royal Sovereign* was intended to be a seagoing ship, as was shown by her folding bulwarks. Her hull and deck were strengthened but not heavily armoured and she was fitted with a twin and three single 265mm/10.5in guns firing solid shot, later replaced by more effective 230mm/9in muzzle-loaders. Because of Cowper Coles's agitation, the Royal Navy also built the slightly smaller *Prince Albert* from scratch, with four 230mm/9in muzzle-loaders. Soon, however, the Royal Navy abandoned this line of development.

The Brazilian navy built a number of coast defence battleships, but only the low-freeboard, twin-turreted, French-built *Javary* and *Solimoes* had battleship-sized guns. The small Argentine navy possessed two low-freeboard monitors, *La Plata* and *Los Andes* (1874), with a narrow superstructure fore and aft that allowed end-on fire. *Almirante Brown* (1880) was built to an antiquated design with a central battery and single turrets fore and aft mounting eight 205mm/8in guns, which were replaced in 1897/8 with 265mm/10.5in guns.

In Sweden the coast defence ships *Svea, Göta* and *Thule* (1886–93) had 255mm/10in guns in a twin turret and *Thule* had a ram, while *Oden, Thor* and *Niord* (1897–9) had 255mm/10in guns in single turrets. Between 1900 and 1905, the Swedish navy built three more classes armed with 210mm/8.3in guns: *Dristigheten* (1900), four ships of the Äran class (1902–4) and *Oscar II* (1905).

Denmark competed with an unusual design, *Helgoland* (1878), a coast defence battleship with a single 305mm/12in gun and four 260mm/10.2in guns, and *Iver Hvitfeldt* (1886) with two 260mm//10.2in guns. Norway and the Netherlands also built several coast defence ships with guns under 255mm/10in. Austro-Hungary built *Monarch, Wien* and *Budapest* (1893), though these were too small to be effective battleships.

The coast defence ship in all its forms was, however, a byway in the development of the battleship.

BELOW: The German *Siegfried* photographed in 1889 mimicked the French design, but being larger also supported a forecastle mounting. The German Kaiser's navy began a period of rapid expansion, turning itself from a coast defence navy into a high seas fleet which would eventually challenge the Royal Navy.

Royal Sovereign class

Under the Naval Defence Act of 1889, £21 million was provided for the construction of ten battleships, 42 cruisers and other vessels over the next five years. The two-power standard whereby the Royal Navy would be maintained at strength equal to two other foreign powers was also endorsed: the enemies then were France and Russia.

The launch and completion of the seven ships of the Royal Sovereign class in just two years was itself an important message. Designed by Sir Samuel White, they were the most powerful battleships in the world, setting new benchmarks in firepower, armour and speed.

White's design was for an enlarged Admiral class barbette ship. The Royal Navy wanted better seakeeping than previous generations of low-freeboard ships. The armoured belt covered two-thirds of the ship's length and was up to 460mm/18in thick and the gun mountings were pear-shaped with 430mm/17in armour. The areas behind the main and

upper belts of armour were used as coalbunkers for additional protection. To save weight the 340mm/13.5in breech-loading guns remained in barbettes. The freeboard was raised to 5.5m/18ft by building another full-length deck, and the armour extended to cover the barbettes and a heavier secondary armament. On build, they were found to roll heavily but after bilge keels were fitted proved to be good sea-keepers capable of maintaining high speeds.

Such a large class meant that their effectiveness was increased by operating in squadrons. Few ships of this class, however, saw active service. The Royal Sovereigns were deployed in the Channel and Mediterranean Fleets, but after 1902 they served exclusively in home waters. From 1907 onwards, when superseded by the Dreadnoughts, the Royal Sovereigns were placed in reserve and most were scrapped by 1914. Only *Revenge* saw service in World War I, when she was deployed on the Belgian

ABOVE: **A coloured postcard of *Empress of India* (1891) dressed overall. The launch of seven ships of the same class in just two years was intended as a strong message to the world.**

coast to give fire-support to the army in 1914–15. Following this she was renamed *Redoubtable* and made a tender to HMS *Victory* until 1919.

Royal Sovereign class

Class: *Royal Sovereign, Empress of India, Ramillies, Repulse, Resolution, Royal Oak, Revenge.*
Launched 1891–2
Dimensions: Length – 115.8m/380ft
Beam – 22.9m/75ft
Draught – 8.4m/27ft 6in
Displacement: 14,377 tonnes/14,150 tons
Armament: Main – 4 x 340mm/13.5in guns
Secondary – 10 x 150mm/6in, 16 x 6-pdr, 12 x 3-pdr guns and 7 x 455mm/18in torpedoes
Machinery: 2 shafts, 8 boilers, 6,711kW/9,000ihp
Performance: 18 knots
Complement: 712 men

Hood

The debate about the design of the pre-Dreadnought battleship was not quite decided, and, under the Naval Defence Act of 1889, an eighth battleship was built, *Hood*. Although a sister ship to the Royal Sovereign battleships and sharing many features of their internal layout, she retained more of the characteristics of an earlier type, the turret ship.

Hood had similar machinery, armour and guns to the Royal Sovereign class, but instead of barbettes, she was fitted with turrets. The greater weight of the turrets meant that these had to be mounted one deck lower. In consequence *Hood* shipped water in even the slightest seaway and so could not maintain such high speeds as her half-sisters.

The design allowed direct comparison between the old and the new concepts, but was not a success. *Hood* saw service briefly in the Mediterranean but was soon withdrawn, used as a receiving ship and then for trials from 1911–14.

LEFT: *Hood* was the eighth battleship to be built under the Naval Defence Act of 1889. The weight of the turrets required them to be carried lower in the ship, and the value of a high freeboard for ships of an ocean-going navy like the Royal Navy was not as widely accepted as it should have been.

Hood became part of the Royal Navy's growing anti-submarine efforts and was the first ship to be fitted with bulges, intended to absorb the impact of a torpedo hit.

Hood

Class: *Hood*. Launched 1891
Dimensions: Length – 125.12m/410ft 6in
  Beam – 22.86m/75ft
  Draught – 8.38m/27ft 6in
Displacement: 14,377 tonnes/14,150 tons
Armament: Main – 4 x 340mm/13.5in guns
  Secondary – 10 x 150mm/6in, 10 x 6pdr,
  12 x 3pdr guns and 5 x 455mm/18in torpedoes
Machinery: 8 boilers, 2 shafts,
  9,000kW/16,000ihp
Performance: 16.7 knots
Complement: 690 men

Renown

Similar in armament to earlier Royal Sovereigns, *Renown* was 2,032 tonnes/2,000 tons heavier than *Centurion* and because she was beamier drew slightly less water. Her increased size was due to her heavier armour, a

Renown

Class: *Renown*. Launched 1895
Dimensions: Length – 124.34m/408ft
  Beam – 22m/72ft
  Draught – 8.15m/26ft 9in
Displacement: 12,548 tonnes/12,350 tons
Armament: Main – 4 x 255mm/10in guns
  Secondary – 10 x 150mm/6in, 12 x 12pdr,
  12 x 3pdr guns and 5 x 455mm/18in torpedoes
Machinery: 8 boilers, 2 shafts.
  6,711kW/9,000ihp
Performance: 17.5 knots
Complement: 674 men

trend which every successor ship followed until the battlecruisers were built. The outer edge of the protective armoured deck over the citadel was also sloped to deflect any shells which might penetrate the belt. She was flagship on the North America and West Indies station from 1897–9, and in the Mediterranean from 1899–1902. With her 150mm/6in guns removed, she carried the Duke and Duchess of Connaught and Prince and Princess of Wales on state visits to India. The role of royal (or presidential) yacht was frequently allotted to battleships.

RIGHT: *Renown* was a handsome, comfortable ship much in demand by admirals as a flagship or as a royal yacht. She saw service in the Atlantic and Indian Oceans, the West Indies and Mediterranean.

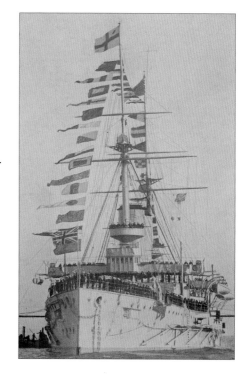

Centurion and *Barfleur*

*C*enturion and *Barfleur* were the smallest of the British pre-Dreadnoughts and officially rated as second-class battleships. Their size enabled them to enter the major Chinese rivers. Although they could not stand up to other, larger Russian and Japanese ships, they could run down any armoured cruiser and as such, they might be regarded as the first battlecruisers.

A revolving armoured hood covered circular barbettes, marking an intermediate stage in the development of the turret. Both ships could reach 17 knots, and slightly higher speeds with forced draught. Both ships were reconstructed in 1901–4 when the 120mm/4.7in guns were replaced with the more usual 150mm/6in ordnance.

Both *Centurion*, which saw service on the China station between 1894 and 1905, and *Barfleur*, which served in the Mediterranean from 1895–8 and then on the China station until 1902, were recalled to home waters after Fisher's redeployment of the British fleet.

Centurion class

Class: *Centurion, Barfleur.* Launched 1892–4
Dimensions: Length – 109.73m/360ft
   Beam – 21.3m/70ft
   Draught – 7.8m/25ft 6in
Displacement: 10,668 tonnes/10,500 tons
Armament: Main – 4 x 255mm/10in guns
   Secondary – 10 x 120mm/4.7in, 8 x 6pdr,
   12 x 3pdr guns and 7 x 455mm/18in torpedoes
Machinery: 8 boilers, 2 shafts,
   6,710kW/9,000ihp
Performance: 18 knots
Complement: 620 men

LEFT AND BELOW: **The two small battleships of the** *Centurion* **class were specialized ships, intended for work overseas and able to enter China's rivers.** *Barfleur* **is seen here in Mediterranean paint scheme in dry dock (left) and at Malta (below). The twin side-by-side funnels were typical of the era.**

Majestic class

The Majestics were the largest single class of battleships ever built. Combining the successful features of the Royal Sovereigns with the improvements in layout adopted in *Renown*, like their predecessors they were good sea-going boats. The 305mm/12in guns became the British standard and proved superior to the previous 340mm/13.5in guns in everything except weight of shell. The extensive armoured belt was 230mm/9in thick and 305mm/12in to 355mm/14in at the bulkheads and barbettes, where, except for a small number of ready-use rounds, the guns had to be trained fore and aft for loading. The bridge, control tower and foremast were combined in the first six ships. By 1908, all carried some oil fuel in addition to coal, and *Caesar* and *Illustrious* had been fitted with new gun-mountings that enabled all-round loading.

All served in the Channel fleet, except *Victorious,* which served on the China station 1898–1900 and *Majestic*, flagship of the Mediterranean fleet 1895–1903. In World War I *Magnificent, Hannibal* and *Mars* were stripped of their guns, which then armed the Lord Clive class of monitors, and were employed as troopships. *Jupiter* escorted the Russian fleet down the English Channel on its way to defeat at the Battle of Tsushima, and after a period as a gunnery training ship was sent to Archangel as an icebreaker in February 1914, and served in the Far East and Middle East.

Illustrious became an ammunition ship. *Prince George*, which had a lucky escape when a torpedo that struck her off Cape Helles in 1915 failed to explode, and was hit by Turkish gunfire during a bombardment off the Dardanelles, survives as a reef off the Netherlands coast, where she foundered on the way to breakers in Germany in 1921. *Majestic* was sunk by a German U-boat. *Caesar* was one of the few pre-Dreadnoughts to see action after World War I, when she supported British operations in the Black Sea against the Bolsheviks.

LEFT: **Besides war fighting, battleships had a diplomatic purpose in peacetime, and this stern view of *Majestic* and the admiral's gallery hints at the luxury onboard, at least for one man.** ABOVE: **This Majestic class appears more warlike, painted all over in grey. The class survived World War I and individual ships were broken up in the 1920s.**

Majestic class

Class: *Magnificent, Jupiter, Majestic, Prince George, Victorious, Mars, Hannibal, Caesar, Illustrious.* Launched 1894–6

Dimensions: Length – 128.3m/421ft
    Beam – 22.9m/75ft
    Draught – 8.2m/27ft

Displacement: 14,445 tonnes/14,890 tons

Armament: Main – 4 x 305mm/12in guns
    Secondary – 12 x 150mm/6in, 16 x 12pdr,
    12 x 2pdr guns and 5 x 455mm/18in torpedoes

Machinery: 8 boilers, 2 shafts,
    8,950kW/12,000ihp

Performance: 17 knots

Complement: 672 men

All (except *Majestic*) were sold for breaking up in 1921–2.

LEFT: **British design, after a generation of change, was remarkably consistent during the pre-Dreadnought period. The Canopus class were only smaller versions of their predecessors. They saw service worldwide and also proved useful in World War I.** BELOW: **The Canopus class were the same length as the Majestics but had their funnels arranged in-line, and with their tall masts made handsome ships and good seagoing vessels.**

Canopus class

British battleship construction in this period showed a consistency in design, and the Canopus class were smaller and faster versions of the Majestics, designed for the Far East and intended to counter the growing naval power of Japan. New-style Krupp armour maintained protection while reducing the thickness and saving 2,032 tonnes/2,000 tons in weight. However, 25.4mm/1in and 50.8mm/2in deck armour was fitted when it was rumoured that the French were fitting howitzers in their ships.

The Canopus class had all-round loading, like *Caesar* and *Illustrious*, and the last of the class, *Vengeance*, was fitted with improved mountings that could also be loaded at any elevation. She had improved armour, giving her flat-sided mountings a "modern" appearance. All earlier British pre-Dreadnoughts had had side-by-side funnels but this was now abandoned in favour of a fore and aft arrangement. The Belleville water-tube boilers worked at 21.1kgcm/300psi, compared to the 11kgcm/155psi of cylindrical boilers, and on trials developed 10,100kW/13,500hp giving speeds of over 18 knots.

Typical of her class, *Glory* served on the China Station from 1900 until 1905 when the Anglo-Japanese alliance made her presence unnecessary. Refitted in 1907 with magazine cooling and fire control, she served in the Mediterranean fleet and then the reserve fleet. In 1914, she escorted Canadian troops across the Atlantic and was relegated to the North American and West Indies station as flagship. After briefly being guard-ship in Egypt, *Glory* was sent to Archangel to remain there until 1919 and was sold to breakers in 1920.

Ocean took part in operations in the Persian Gulf in October 1914 and was at the Dardanelles on March 18, 1915 when she was damaged by gunfire and then hit a floating mine. After an orderly abandonment, *Ocean* sank three hours later. In November 1914 *Goliath* took part in the operation against the *Königsberg*, a German commerce-raiding cruiser that had taken refuge far up in the Rufiji River in East Africa. She was hit twice by Turkish gunfire off Cape Helles in April and May 1915, and on May 13, she was torpedoed by the Turkish motor torpedo boat *Muavenet* and sank with the loss of 570 men.

Canopus class

Class: *Albion, Glory, Canopus, Goliath, Ocean, Vengeance.* Launched 1897–9
Dimensions: Length – 128.5m/421ft 6in
Beam – 22.6m/74ft
Draught – 8m/26ft 2in
Displacement: 13,360 tonnes/13,150 tons
Armament: Main – 4 x 305mm/12in guns
Secondary – 12 x 150mm/6in, 10 x 12pdr, 6 x 3pdr guns and 4 x 455mm/18in torpedoes
Machinery: 20 Belleville boilers, 2 shafts, 10,100kW/13,500ihp
Performance: 18 knots
Complement: 682 men

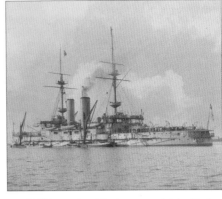

LEFT: **British naval architects were certainly able to design good-looking ships to a classic recipe: two double turrets, two funnels and two pole masts.** ABOVE: **The class continued the gradual evolution of the pre-Dreadnoughts.** BELOW: **Their usefulness continued into the Dreadnought era, although** *Formidable* **was sunk by a U-boat in the English Channel in 1915 and** *Irresistible* **by Turkish mines in 1916, and only** *Implacable* **survived World War I.**

Formidable class

The three ships of this class continued the trend in development of the Majestic and Canopus designs, in which the use of lighter Krupp armour was used to give greater protection rather than to reduce size. Similar to Canopus, the armour belt was extended to the stern and bow. The armament was also similar to the earlier ships, but of larger calibre, and, like *Vengeance*, the 305mm/12in guns could be loaded on any bearing and elevation. To achieve this, a deep hoist opened into a working chamber beneath the guns, which also reduced the possibility of fire or blast spreading to the magazines.

They were fitted with inward-turning propellers resulting in improved speed (over 18 knots) and reduced fuel consumption, but at slow speeds they were difficult to manoeuvre.

All served in the Mediterranean from commissioning until 1908, when they were withdrawn to home waters, fitted with fire control and an array of wireless aerials. *Formidable* had been paid-off into the reserve when World War I broke out, and she was sunk on January 1, 1915, while unescorted on passage in Lyme Bay west of Portland Bill. Struck by torpedoes from the German submarine *U-24,* she sank with heavy loss of life in the cold and darkness, and bad weather.

These pre-Dreadnoughts were not fit to fight in the main theatre of operations, the North Sea, and were relegated to secondary operations such as the landings at Gallipoli, where *Irresistible* was mined and sunk on March 18, 1915. The Turks had covertly laid an extra row of mines where the allies attempted to execute a plan to force their way through to Constantinople. The mines also trapped *Ocean* and the French battleship *Bouvet*: of 16 British and French battleships that took part in the attempt to rush the straits, three were badly damaged and three were sunk. *Ocean* and *Bouvet* sank in minutes, while

Irresistible took several hours to sink and was only saved from drifting on to the shore of Turkey by the strong stream emerging from the Bosporus.

Formidable class

Class: *Formidable, Irresistible, Implacable.*
  Launched 1898–9
Dimensions: Length – 131.6m/431ft 9in
  Beam – 22.86m/75ft
  Draught – 7.9m/25ft 11in
Displacement: 14,733 tonnes/14,500 tons
Armament: Main – 4 x 305mm/12in guns
  Secondary – 12 x 150mm/6in, 16 x 12pdr,
  6 x 3pdr guns and 4 x 455mm/18in torpedoes
Machinery: 20 Belleville boilers, 2 shafts,
  11,190kW/15,000ihp
Performance: 18 knots
Complement: 780 men
Implacable was broken up in 1921.

LEFT: *London* in camouflage and fitted as a minelayer. Her heavy guns were removed and she could carry an outfit of 240 mines. The dazzle patterns were meant to prevent U-boat commanders from achieving a torpedo-firing solution by accurate estimation of speed and course. BELOW: One of the newly completed London class entering Malta very early in the 20th century.

London class

The first three ships of the London class were constructed under the 1898–9 naval estimates and the last two under the 1900–1 estimates. They were largely repeats of the Formidable class with some changes to their armour, which included a longer armoured belt. All had Belleville boilers, except *Queen,* which was fitted with Babcock and Wilcox boilers. The designed displacement was 15,240 tonnes/15,000 tons although there was some variation across the class.

Venerable served in the Mediterranean and then in home waters.

Bulwark was an ill-fated ship. Intended as flagship of the Mediterranean Fleet, delays in her refit meant she joined the Home Fleet instead. In October 1907, she grounded needing repairs. While loading ammunition at Sheerness on November 26, 1914, she was destroyed by a massive internal explosion, with only a dozen survivors from her complement of over 700 officers and men. The cause was widely attributed to the unstable nature of the black powder in use, which destroyed several ships of this epoch.

London was flagship of the Channel Fleet in 1908 and of the Atlantic Fleet in 1910. In 1912, she was used in flying experiments, which included the first take-off from a ship underway, using a 7.3m/24ft ramp built out over a turret and used to launch a biplane. At the outbreak of war she was employed on Channel patrols until sent on the Dardanelles expedition. Transferred to the Adriatic in May 1915, she was based at Taranto until 1917. Her 305mm/12in guns were removed and the after-gun replaced with a 150mm/6in gun when she became a minelayer, carrying 240 mines.

Queen and *Prince of Wales* differed from the rest of the London class by having open 12pdr gun batteries amidships. Like *London,* both ships were engaged on Channel patrols before being sent to support the ANZAC landings at Gallipoli, and were then based at Taranto, partly to check the Austro-Hungarian fleet in the Adriatic. *Queen*'s 305mm/12in guns were removed in Italy and transferred to the Italian Navy in 1918. All were sold for breaking up in 1920.

London class

Class: *London, Bulwark, Venerable, Queen, Prince of Wales.* Launched 1899–1902
Dimensions: Length – 131.6m/431ft 9in
 Beam – 22.86m/75ft in
 Draught – 7.92m/26ft
Displacement: 14,733 tonnes/14,500 tons
Armament: Main – 4 x 305mm/12in guns
 Secondary – 12 x 150mm/6in, 16 x 12pdr,
 6 x 3pdr guns and 4 x 455mm/18in torpedoes
Machinery: 20 boilers, 2 shafts,
 11,190kW/15,000ihp
Performance: 18 knots
Complement: 714 men

LEFT: The battleship *Russell* in the 1900s. She has an extensive suite of radio aerials but no range-finding equipment to enable her to fire her heavy guns accurately at long range. BELOW: Though only a few years old, the Duncan class were made immediately obsolete by the Dreadnought revolution. *Albemarle*, seen here, was used as an icebreaker in World War I. BELOW LEFT: An evocative picture of the Duncans at sea and working as a homogenous squadron.

Duncan class

Four ships were ordered in 1898 in response to a perceived threat from France and Russia, and two more in 1899. Designed before the London class, and intended to catch fast Russian battleships, the Duncan class sacrificed armour for speed. The armour of the belts and around the barbettes was thinner than the Londons, and speed came from four extra boilers and a modified hull form. They were the first British battleships to exceed 19 knots. The Duncans operated in the Mediterranean until 1904–5 and then in home waters, with the exception of *Duncan, Exmouth* and *Russell,* which also served in the Mediterranean from 1908 until 1912.

Albemarle saw service in the Channel and Atlantic Fleets, and was flagship at Gibraltar until she became a gunnery tender in May 1913. At the outbreak of World War I she served on the Northern Patrol, the distant blockade of Germany where in November 1915 she was badly damaged by heavy weather while in the Pentland Firth. After repairs, she served as an icebreaker at Archangel, and after having her guns stripped out she became an accommodation ship at Devonport in 1917.

Cornwallis was the first ship to open fire in the Dardanelles, on February 18, 1915, and she took part in all the operations including the evacuation of troops from the peninsula. She was hit by three torpedoes from German U-boat *U-32* on January 9, 1917 and sank about 100km/60 miles south-east of Malta with the loss of 15 lives.

Exmouth and *Russell* bombarded Zeebrugge in November 1914 and again in May 1915, and both served in the Dardanelles. *Exmouth* returned to Britain and was paid-off in 1917, but *Russell* was mined, reputedly by the German U-boat *U-72*, on April 27, 1916, just off the coast of Malta with the loss of over 100 lives.

Montagu ran aground on Lundy on May 30, 1906, and was wrecked, although her guns were later salvaged.

The surviving ships were sold for scrap in 1920.

Duncan class

Class: *Duncan, Cornwallis, Exmouth, Montagu, Russell, Albemarle.* Launched 1901
Dimensions: Length – 131.7m/432ft
   Beam – 23m/75ft 6in
   Draught – 7.9m/25ft 9in
Displacement: 13,482 tonnes/13,270 tons
Armament: Main – 4 x 305mm/12in guns
   Secondary – 12 x 150mm/6in, 10 x 12pdr,
   6 x 3pdr guns and 4 x 455mm/18in torpedoes
Machinery: 24 Belleville boilers, 2 shafts,
   13,429kW/18,000ihp
Performance: 19 knots
Complement: 720 men

LEFT: **The King Edward VII class or "The Wobbly Eight" were so-called because, although very manoeuvrable ships, the design of their underwater form and balanced rudders caused lateral instability. Completed during and after the Dreadnought revolution, they were workhorses of the fleet.** ABOVE: **When modernized with torpedo bulges and improved fire-control (on tripod masts) they saw action throughout World War I.** BELOW: **Note the funnel bands painted so that one ship could be distinguished from another.**

King Edward VII class

Ordered in three batches between 1901 and 1903, the King Edward VII class marked a departure from the Majestic class derivatives. Their armament including four 235mm/9.2in guns mounted in single turrets on the upper deck and the 150mm/6in casement guns were moved up one deck to a central battery behind 180mm/7in armoured bulkheads. In consequence they were criticized because, not having a uniform secondary armament, it was almost impossible to distinguish between the fall of shot of various guns which prevented good fire control. Completed with fighting tops on pole masts, these were replaced by fire-control platforms on tripod masts.

In the battle of the boilers, the class was fitted with various steam plants. They were also the first British pre-Dreadnoughts to be fitted with balanced rudders, and though this gave them a small turning circle at speed, they had difficulty keeping a steady course and earned the name "The Wobbly Eight".

Most ships served prior to World War I in the Atlantic, Channel and Home Fleets and formed a single unit, the Third Battle Squadron, from May 1912 onwards. In August 1914, the Third Battle Squadron joined the Grand Fleet at Scapa Flow. Towards the end of the war, they were partially reconstructed, given anti-torpedo bulges and a tripod mast with director control platforms, and the 150mm/6in battery was replaced with four 150mm/6in guns placed one deck higher.

King Edward VII served briefly pre-war in the Mediterranean, but after she joined the Third Battle Squadron, was mined off Cape Wrath. Both engine rooms flooded and *King Edward VII* capsized and sank after 12 hours. *Commonwealth* distinguished herself by colliding with the battleship *Albemarle* in 1907 and in the same year by going aground.

The Royal Navy's interest in aviation was highlighted when in May 1912, *Hibernia* was fitted with a 30.5m/100ft-long runway over the forecastle and Commander Sampson made the first ever flight from a British ship, on May 4, 1912. All were culled after the Washington Naval Treaty, along with scores of other battleships in the world's navies, most of them of prewar design.

King Edward VII class

Class: *King Edward VII, Commonwealth, Dominion, Hindustan, New Zealand, Britannia, Hibernia, Africa.* Launched 1903–5
Dimensions: Length – 138.3m/453ft 9in
  Beam – 23.8m/78ft
  Draught – 7.8m/25ft 8in
Displacement: 15,835 tonnes/15,585 tons
Armament: Main – 4 x 305mm/12in and
  4 x 235mm/9.2in guns
  Secondary – 10 x 150mm/6in, 14 x 12pdr,
  14 x 3pdr guns and 4 x 455mm/18in torpedoes
Machinery: 10, 12 or 16 boilers, 2 shafts,
  13,420kW/18,000ihp
Speed: 18.5 knots
Complement: 777 men
  New Zealand was renamed *Zealandia* in 1911.
  King Edward VII was fitted with 10 Babcock and
  Wilcox boilers, *Dominion* and *Commonwealth*
  with 16 Babcock and Wilcox, *New Zealand* with
  12 Niclausse; the others 12 Babcock and Wilcox.

LEFT: The Royal Navy bought the two ships of the Swiftsure class, while under construction, from the Chilean navy in order to end an arms race in South America. *Triumph* (formerly *Libertad*) is seen at anchor at a fleet review.

Swiftsure class

Class: *Swiftsure* (ex *Constitucion*), *Triumph* (ex *Libertad*). Launched 1903
Dimensions: Length – 146.2m/479ft 9in
Beam – 21.6m/71ft
Draught – 7.7m/25ft 4in
Displacement: 11,990 tonnes/11,800 tons
Armament: Main – 4 x 255mm/10in and 14 x 190mm/7.5in guns
Secondary – 14 x 14pdr, 2 x 12pdr guns and 2 x 455mm/18in torpedoes
Machinery: 12 large-tube Yarrow boilers, 2 shafts, 10,490kW/12,500ihp
Speed: 19 knots
Complement: 800 men

Swiftsure class

Chile has long-standing connections with Britain, and it was in Chile's independence struggle that Lord Cochrane repeated and exceeded some of his exploits when he had fought the French and Spanish in the Great War of 1793–1815. Independence did not mean peace and Chile and its neighbours fought a series of wars and civil wars. During a war with Peru, the turret ship *Huascar* was captured in 1879, and so has been preserved. At a battle in 1891, during a revolution in which the Chilean

forces supported the forces for change, the government torpedo gunboat *Almirante Lynch* sank the protected cruiser *Blanco Encalada*: this was the first successful use of a self-propelled torpedo against an armoured vessel.

In the 1890s Chile had ordered some ships from France, but when a border dispute threatened war with Argentina, Chile ordered two battleships from Britain: *Constitucion* and *Libertad*, designed by Sir Edward Reed. They were still building when the crisis in South

America was settled, and the Royal Navy, which reckoned ships under construction for other governments formed a reserve, bought them both and they were re-named *Swiftsure* and *Triumph*. This also stopped the Russians from acquiring these ships for its war with Japan.

In comparison with other British ships, *Swiftsure* and *Triumph* were lightly armoured and lightly armed, and their beam and draught, limited by the size of Chilean docks, made them relatively long, thin and fast. Despite their powerful secondary armament, they were rated as second-class battleships. If they could not stand up to battleships, they could certainly run down and out-gun any cruiser or merchant ship and so, by 1913, *Swiftsure* became flagship of the East Indies station and *Triumph* had been sent to the China station. *Swiftsure* was scrapped in 1920, but *Triumph* was torpedoed by *U-21* off the Dardanelles on May 25, 1915.

LEFT: These were small battleships by the Royal Navy's contemporary standards and were going to replace *Centurion* and *Barfleur* on the China station, but they were both recalled to the Dardanelles.

Lord Nelson class

The Lord Nelsons were provided under the 1904/5 Estimates, and had a designed displacement of 16,765 tonnes/16,500 tons. The progress towards a heavier armament, first seen in *King Edward VII*, was taken a stage further in this design; all 150mm/6in guns were abandoned in favour of a complete secondary battery of 235mm/9.2in guns all mounted in turrets. This disposed of the unsatisfactory main deck batteries that, despite their limitations, had been repeated in every class since the Royal Sovereigns. The only other gun armament was 12pdr for torpedo boat defence, and these were mounted on a flying deck over an amidships structure reminiscent of Reed's turret ships. Owing to the limited space for shrouds, a tripod mainmast was adopted. The vessels were slightly heavier than the King Edward VIIs but docking restrictions required that their length be limited, so beam and draught were increased, and a squarer hull form amidships allowed some fining of the lines fore and aft to give a speed of 18 knots. They were good sea-boats and gun-platforms and had exceptional manoeuvrability. On trials, *Lord Nelson* made 18.7 knots with 13,008kW/17,445ihp and *Agamemnon* 18.5 knots with 12,878kW/17,270ihp.

In the long term, they were not successful ships because of the fire control problems with mixed-calibre armament. Their 305mm/12in guns were

new pattern 45-calibre weapons; the guns and mountings originally ordered for them were used in the *Dreadnought* and their completion was delayed while replacement guns were manufactured.

The waterline armour belt extended over the full length of the hull and was 305mm/12in amidships reducing to 230mm/9in and 150mm/6in forward and 100mm/4in aft. The upper belt extended from the stern to the after barbette only, and was 205mm/8in amidships reducing to 150mm/6in and 100mm/4in forward and closed by a 205mm/8in bulkhead at the after end. Between the upper belt

ABOVE: **It was the mixed armament of 305mm/12in and 235mm/9.2in guns, clearly seen here in *Lord Nelson*, photographed in 1917 at Malta, which made these ships pre-Dreadnoughts.** BELOW: ***Agamemnon* bringing up the rear of the British line of battle.**

and upper deck the bases of the 235mm/9.2in mountings were protected by a citadel of uniform 205mm/8in armour extending from forward to aft barbette.

Lord Nelson began her career as flagship of the Fifth Battle Squadron in the Channel Fleet, and in 1915 was sent to the Mediterranean. There she took part in the Dardanelles campaign, in which she hit and was hit by Turkish batteries, but sustained only light damage. She was kept in the eastern Mediterranean to bottle up the German *Goeben* and finally entered the Black Sea in November 1918. *Agamemnon* operated closely with *Lord Nelson*: together they destroyed Kavak Bridge in December 1915 and on October 30, 1918, the Turkish armistice was signed onboard *Agamemnon*, before both ships passed through the Dardanelles.

Lord Nelson class

Class: *Lord Nelson, Agamemnon.* Launched 1906
Dimensions: Length – 135.2m/443ft 6in
  Beam – 24.2m/79ft 6in
  Draught – 7.9m/26ft
Displacement: 16,348 tonnes/16,090 tons
Armament: Main – 4 x 305mm/12in and
  10 x 235mm/9.2in guns
  Secondary – 24 x 12pdr, 2 x 3pdr guns
  and 5 x 455mm/18in torpedoes
Machinery: 15 boilers, 2 shafts,
  12,490kW/16,750ihp
Speed: 18 knots
Complement: 800 men

LEFT: **Spain was wrongly blamed for the loss of USS *Maine* in 1898. Twentieth-century scientific investigation suggested an innocent explanation but the USA was looking for an excuse for war.**

Maine

Maine	
Class: *Maine*. Launched 1889	
Dimensions: Length – 97.23m/319ft	
Beam – 17.37m/57ft	
Draught – 6.55m/21ft 6in	
Displacement: 6,789 tonnes/6,682 tons	
Armament: Main – 4 x 255mm/10in and	
6 x 150mm/6in guns	
Secondary – 7 x 6pdr, 8 x 1pdr guns and	
4 x 355mm/14in torpedoes	
Machinery: 4 boilers, 2 shafts, 6710kW/9,000ihp	
Speed: 17 knots	
Complement: 374 men	

Authorized in 1886, *Maine* rated as a second-class battleship, forming part of the USN's North Atlantic Squadron when she was sent to Havana, Cuba, to protect American property and life during a revolutionary struggle against Spain.

On February 15, 1898, shortly before 22.00, an explosion tore *Maine* apart, shattering the forward part of the ship, sinking her and killing 260 officers and men. Although an official report concluded that Spain (then the colonial power in Cuba) could not definitely be blamed for the disaster, the USA was stirred into frenzy and two months later "Remember the *Maine*" became the war cry that started the Spanish-American War. *Maine* was raised and towed out to be sunk in the Gulf of Mexico in 1912. Her mainmast is in Arlington National Cemetery and her mizzenmast at the US Naval Academy, Annapolis.

Several ships of this era blew up suddenly, this usually being blamed on unstable ammunition, but in 1976 Admiral Hyman Rickover conducted a new investigation and decided that the cause was spontaneous combustion in *Maine*'s coalbunkers.

Texas

Part of the American flying squadron that blockaded Cienfuegos, Cuba, in May 1898, *Texas* later reconnoitred Guantanamo Bay. On June 16, she bombarded Cayo del Tore, destroying a fort there from 1,280m/1,400 yards' range in an hour and a quarter.

On May 19, a Spanish squadron under Admiral Pascual Cervera arrived in Santiago harbour on the southern coast of Cuba. While North American troops landed, a USN fleet blockaded the harbour. (These troops included the Rough Riders, a volunteer cavalry regiment led by Theodore Roosevelt who would subsequently do so much to advance the USN.) When the Spanish attempted to break out of Santiago, an unequal fight took place on July 3, 1898, known as the Battle of Santiago, between the Spanish squadron of cruisers and destroyers and the USN flying squadron that included the battleships *Texas, Indiana* and *Oregon*.

The Spanish fleet was annihilated, sealing the fate of the last Spanish colony in the Americas. *Texas* was expended as a target in 1911–12.

LEFT: **These small (6,095 tonnes/6,000 tons) ships suggest that the USN was not yet thinking in oceanic terms, though when war broke out with Spain they proved useful in the Caribbean.**

Texas	
Class: *Texas*. Launched 1889	
Dimensions: Length – 94.1m/308ft 10in	
Beam – 19.4m/64ft	
Draught – 6.9m/22ft 6in	
Displacement: 5,728 tonnes/6,316 tons	
Armament: Main – 2 x 305mm/12in and	
6 x 100mm/4in guns	
Secondary – 12 x 6pdr, 6 x 1pdr guns and	
4 x 355mm/14in torpedoes	
Machinery: 4 boilers, 2 shafts,	
5,900kW/8,600ihp	
Speed: 17 knots	
Complement: 392/508 men	

Indiana class

Indiana was initially designated "BB1" but she and her sisters were later re-rated as coast battleships. Although larger than previous designs, they were over-armed and had only 3.35m/11ft freeboard. *Indiana* and *Massachusetts* were sunk as targets in the early 1920s while *Oregon* became a museum ship until 1942, an ammunition carrier in 1944, and was finally sold for breaking up in 1956.

During the Spanish-American War *Indiana* was deployed to intercept Cervera's Spanish squadron, which wild invasion rumours alleged was going to steam up the Potomac. *Indiana* did not join in the first phase of the Battle of Santiago, but when the Spanish destroyers *Pluton* and *Furor* emerged from harbour, she overwhelmed them.

Indiana made several training cruises carrying midshipmen of the US Naval Academy, which included a visit to Queenstown, Ireland, when she fired a 21-gun salute for the coronation of King George V. She served during World War I as a gunnery training ship, and afterwards served as a target for aerial bombs, was sunk in 1920 and sold for scrap in 1924. *Massachusetts* also blockaded Cuba,

although she missed the Battle of Santiago. However, she helped force the unarmoured cruiser *Reina Mercedes* ashore on July 6, 1898. Afterwards she served in the USN's North Atlantic Squadron and as a training ship. Scuttled off Pensacola Bar, she was declared Florida state property in 1956.

Oregon was slightly larger than her sisters. On her 22,530km/14,000-mile maiden voyage from San Francisco to Jupiter Point, Florida, to join the fleet assembling for the attack on Cuba, she demonstrated both the capability of the USN to deploy its ships, and the need for the Panama Canal. After the Battle of Santiago, *Oregon* was sent to the USN's Asiatic station. She cooperated with the US army in the Philippine insurrection, and was sent to Taku during the Boxer Rebellion in China. However, on June 28, 1900, she grounded on a rock in the

Straits of Pechili, and was nearly wrecked. In June 1925 she was loaned to the State of Oregon as a floating museum. At Guam in 1948 she broke her moorings during a typhoon and was found some days later 805km/500 miles away. She was finally scrapped in Japan.

Indiana class

Class: *Indiana, Massachusetts, Oregon.*
  Launched 1893
Dimensions: Length – 106.95m/350ft 11in
  Beam – 21.1m/69ft 3in
  Draught – 7.3m/24ft
Displacement: 10,498 tonnes/10,288 tons
Armament: Main – 4 x 330mm/13in and
  8 x 205mm/8in guns
  Secondary – 20 x 6pdr, 6 x 1pdr guns and
  6 x 455mm/18in torpedoes
Machinery: 6 boilers, 2 shafts, 6,710kW/9,000ihp
Speed: 15 knots
Complement: 473 men

BELOW: **The Indiana class (10,160 tonnes/10,000 tons) was able to deploy within the American hemisphere, from California to Florida, in time to influence the outcome of the war.** RIGHT: **Officially rated as BB-1, the size of *Indiana* is indicated by the sailors standing atop one of the 205mm/8in, side-mounted gun turrets in the 1890s.**

Iowa

The second ship of her name in the USN, *Iowa* served in the Atlantic Fleet. She fired the first shots in the Battle of Santiago on July 3, 1898, and overwhelmed the Spanish cruisers *Infanta Maria Teresa* and *Oquendo* in a one-sided 20-minute fight, setting both ships on fire and driving them ashore. *Iowa* rescued the survivors of these ships and of the cruisers and two other destroyers, including the Spanish commander, Admiral Cervera. The battle, which was the highlight of *Iowa*'s career, was not a true test of her design. After Cuba gained its independence, *Iowa* spent two and a half years in the Pacific, and in 1902 she became flagship of the USN South Atlantic Squadron.

Her subsequent career was typical of many of the USN pre-Dreadnoughts, few of which were seriously tested in battle. She was decommissioned in June 1903, recommissioned on December 23, 1903, and joined the North Atlantic Squadron to participate in the John Paul Jones Commemoration ceremonies in June 1905. *Iowa* was placed in reserve in July 1907, and decommissioned at Philadelphia in July 1908. She was rearmed in 1909 and, in additon to her military or pole foremast, was given a cage or lattice mainmast.

When recommissioned again in May 1910, *Iowa* served as a training ship in the Atlantic Reserve Fleet, making a number of training cruises to northern Europe, and she participated in the naval review at Philadelphia in October 1912. She saw limited service in World War I, first as a receiving ship, then as a training ship, and finally, when the USA had entered the war, as a guard ship in Chesapeake Bay. She was finally decommissioned on March 31, 1919.

TOP: *Iowa* in the white and buff paint scheme, similar to the Royal Navy's, which later gave the name to the "Great White Fleet". ABOVE: **After World War I, *Iowa* was stripped of her guns and became a radio-controlled target ship used in bombing experiments.** BELOW LEFT: **Most large ships of the period carried complements of marines, and here US marines are seen at drill onboard *Iowa*.**

Iowa

Class: *Iowa*. Launched 1896
Dimensions: Length – 110.5m/362ft 5in
  Beam – 22m/72ft 3in
  Draught – 7.3m/24ft
Displacement: 11,593 tonnes/11,410 tons
Armament: Main – 4 x 305mm/12in and
  8 x 205mm/8in guns
  Secondary – 6 x 100mm/4in, 20 x 6-pdr guns
  and 4 x 355mm/14in torpedoes
Machinery: 5 boilers, 2 shafts, 8,900kW/11,000ihp
Speed: 16 knots
Complement: 486/654 men

LEFT: **Besides the Dreadnought revolution, there were other new weapons like the submarine. Here *Kearsarge* and an early USN submarine inspect each other, in about 1898.** BELOW: ***Kearsarge* was retrofitted with lattice or cage masts. The distribution of weight helped to reduce vibration in the spotting tops at the head of the masts and so improved the performance of optical rangefinders.**

Kearsarge class

USN battleships were named after the states of the Union, except *Kearsarge*, which took her name from a steam sloop of the American Civil War that sank the Confederate raider *Alabama* off Cherbourg in 1864.

Kearsarge was flagship of the North Atlantic Station in 1903 and again in 1904. As flagship of the USN European Squadron, the German Kaiser visited her on June 26, 1903 at Kiel and the Prince of Wales on July 13 at Spithead. When the North Atlantic Battleship *Squadron* visited Lisbon, she entertained the King of Portugal on June 11, 1904, and on the Fourth of July in Phaleron, she hosted the King, Prince Andrew and Princess Alice of Greece. During target practice off Cape Cruz, Cuba on April 13, 1906, a powder charge ignited in a 330mm/13in gun killing two officers and eight men; four others were seriously injured.

Kearsarge was one of the Great White Fleet of battleships which President Theodore Roosevelt sent around the world in 1907. *Kearsarge* commenced a modernization programme in the Philadelphia Navy Yard in 1909, but she had already been made obsolete by the Dreadnought revolution and was not commissioned again until 1915, when she took US marines to Vera Cruz, Mexico.

Kearsarge was used as a training ship for several years and then converted to a 10,160-tonne/10,000-ton crane ship. She retained her name until it was required for an aircraft carrier in 1941, then becoming a crane ship, and finally she was sold for scrap in 1955.

Fitted out in New York, *Kentucky* sailed via Gibraltar and the Suez Canal to become the flagship on the US Asiatic Station from 1901–4, visiting Hong Kong and the principal ports of China and Japan. She landed marines in Cuba in 1906 to protect American interests and property during an insurrection there and in 1907 was one of 16 battleships in the Great White Fleet.

During 1915 and 1916 *Kentucky* patrolled off Vera Cruz, watching American interests during the Mexican Revolution. Post-war she was used as a training ship, and scrapped in 1924 under the Washington Naval Treaty.

ABOVE: ***Kearsarge* leading ships of the USN's European squadron in review past a line of British battleships (not shown) in 1903. She is followed by two cruisers, *Chicago* and *San Francisco*.**

Kearsarge class

Class: *Kearsarge, Kentucky.* Launched 1898
Dimensions: Length – 114.4m/375ft 4in
    Beam – 22m/72ft 3in
    Draught – 7.16m/23ft 6in
Displacement: 11,725 tonnes/11,540 tons
Armament: Main – 4 x 330mm/13in and
    4 x 205mm/8in guns
    Secondary – 14 x 125mm/5in, 20 x 6pdr guns
    and 4 x 455mm/18in torpedoes
Machinery: 5 boilers, 2 shafts, 7,450kW/10,000ihp
Speed: 16 knots
Complement: 553 men

The 205mm/8in turrets were fitted atop the 330mm/13in turrets and trained together as one unit, an arrangement which did work well. Rearmed in 1909–11, both ships were fitted with cage masts fore and aft.

LEFT AND ABOVE: Like *Kearsarge*, these two pictures show *Wisconsin* as built in the 1900s and *Illinois* (of the same class) after modernization immediately pre-war and in the grey paintwork which the USN adopted after the cruise of the "Great White Fleet". BELOW: A rare picture of the period showing the hull shape of an American pre-Dreadnought – *Illinois* in dry dock in the New Orleans Navy Yard in 1902.

Illinois class

When *Illinois* was flagship of the USN European Squadron, she ran aground off Christiania (now Oslo), Norway, and had to be docked in the Royal Navy dockyard at Chatham in 1902. Like many ships of her vintage she was used as a training ship in World War I. After the war she was laid up until being sold to the state of New York in 1921 for use by the Naval Militia. Demilitarized under the Washington Naval Treaty, *Illinois* was fitted out as a floating armoury in 1924 and became part of the New York Naval Reserve. She remained in New York until 1941, when she was renamed *Prairie State* so that her name could be given to a projected new battleship. In 1956 *Prairie State* was sold for scrap to the Bethlehem Steel Corporation.

From her commissioning in 1901, *Alabama* took part in fleet exercises and gunnery training in the Gulf of Mexico and the West Indies in the wintertime before returning north for repairs and operations off the New England coast during the summer and autumn. Exceptionally, in 1904, *Alabama*, in company with the battleships *Kearsarge*, *Maine* and *Iowa*, visited Portugal and the Mediterranean.

Although *Alabama* started out as part of the Great White Fleet, she was delayed for repairs in San Francisco, and did not visit Japan but, accompanied by the new battleship *Maine*, completed her circumnavigation of the globe via Honolulu and Guam, Manila, Singapore, Colombo, Aden and the Suez Canal.

On return to the USA she was placed in reserve, coming out only to be used for training. Eventually *Alabama* was sunk in Chesapeake Bay in bombing tests by planes of the US Army and her hulk sold for scrap in 1924.

Wisconsin was built on the West Coast and served her early years in the Pacific. In 1902 she hosted peace talks between Panama and Colombia which became known as the "The Peace of Wisconsin". From 1903–6 *Wisconsin* formed part of the USN Asiatic Fleet's Northern Squadron, steaming up the Yangtze River as far as Nanking. After her circumnavigation she remained on the East Coast and after an uneventful career was sold for scrap in 1922.

Illinois class

Class: *Illinois, Alabama, Wisconsin.* Launched 1898
Dimensions: Length – 117.6m/386ft
 Beam – 22m/72ft 3in
 Draught – 7.1m/23ft 5in
Displacement: 11,751 tonnes/11,565 tons
Armament: Main – 4 x 330mm/13in and
 14 x 150mm/6in guns
 Secondary – 16 x 6pdr, 6 x 1pdr guns and
 4 x 455mm/18in torpedoes
Machinery: 6 boilers, 2 shafts,7,450kW//10,000ihp
Speed: 15 knots
Complement: 536 men

The dimensions given are for *Illinois*, but there were small differences between all three ships of this class. An unusual feature of the class was their side-by-side funnels. All three ships formed part of the Great White Fleet.

Maine class

The second *Maine* was laid down in Philadelphia a year to the day after the destruction of the first. She was launched in July 1901 and not commissioned until December 29, 1902. Like others of her vintage, she took part in the Great White Fleet, although in company with *Alabama* took a shorter route and arrived back on the Atlantic coast in October 1908 in advance of the rest of the fleet.

Used as a training ship in World War I, *Maine* took part in the review of the fleet at New York on December 26, 1918.

Maine operated with ships of the Atlantic Fleet until May 15, 1920, when she was decommissioned at Philadelphia Navy Yard.

The distinguishing feature of *Missouri*'s career, while serving in the USN Atlantic Fleet in April 1904, was a flashback from the left gun of her after turret that ignited powder charges in their ready stowage. There was no explosion but the subsequent rapid burning suffocated 36 of the gun's crew. Efficient damage-control measures prevented the spread of fire and by June *Missouri* was repaired and ready for service. An investigation into the cause of the fire led to improvements in the design of the turret and magazine, which were incorporated in the British monitor *Raglan*, which had American built turrets, and when *Raglan* suffered a turret explosion she sank without explosion.

All three ships differed in displacement and *Ohio*, built by the Union Iron Works at San Francisco on the west coast, was the smallest. *Ohio* was flagship of the USN's Asiatic Fleet, and at Manila in April 1905 embarked a party which comprised the Secretary of War William Howard Taft and Alice Roosevelt, the daughter of the president of the USA, for a tour of the Far East that included the Philippines, China and Japan.

Missouri and *Ohio* were also part of the Great White Fleet. All three ships were scrapped under the Washington Naval Treaty.

Maine class

Class: *Maine, Missouri, Ohio.* Launched 1901
Dimensions: Length – 120.1m/393ft 11in
  Beam – 22m/72ft 3in
  Draught – 7.4m/24ft 4in
Displacement: 13,052 tonnes/12,846 tons
Armament: Main – 4 x 305mm/12in and
  16 x 150mm/6in guns
  Secondary – 6 x 75mm/3in, 8 x 8pdrs guns and
  2 x 455mm/18in torpedoes
Machinery: 12 boilers, 2 shafts,
  11,930kW/16,000ihp
Speed: 18 knots
Complement: 561 men

LEFT: **After her loss in 1898, *Maine* was immediately replaced by a new pre-Dreadnought and sister ship to *Missouri* and *Ohio*.** BELOW LEFT: **A close-up of the forward 305mm/12in gun mounting in *Ohio*.**
BELOW: ***Missouri* was modernized pre-war with cage masts, fighting tops and turret-mounted rangefinders.**

59

LEFT: *Rhode Island* photographed off New York in 1909, clearly showing the superimposed turrets. Also the forward pole mast has been replaced by a lattice with searchlight platforms. ABOVE: *Nebraska*, before acceptance into the USN, making smoke and a bow wave while undergoing speed trials. BELOW: Sailors and marines in *Virginia* with something to cheer. Note the field gun in its component parts on the deck.

Virginia class

The largest single class of USN pre-Dreadnoughts was authorized in 1889 and 1900. They were larger again than their predecessors and, in spite of the unsatisfactory experience in *Kearsarge* and *Kentucky*, the superimposed turret arrangement was repeated. There were more than half a dozen different calibres of guns, with all the problems of ammunition supply and spotting fall of shot. When refitted in 1909–10, the 150mm/6in guns were removed, and the number of 75mm/3in guns reduced. At the same time the pole masts were replaced by cages. On trials, they were the first USN battleships to exceed 19 knots.

Virginia's career in Cuba, The Great White Fleet, in Europe and Mexico was unexceptional. However, coal supplies had been a problem during the fleet's circumnavigation and in 1910, *Virginia* experimented with equipment for coaling at sea. She was in refit at Boston when World War I broke out and her crew were employed boarding interned German merchant ships. *Virginia* made eight

trooping voyages, more than any other battleship, from France in 1918 and 1919. She was expended as a target. *Virginia* and *New Jersey* were bombed at anchor by the US Army. The trials were artificial, but gave a significant impetus to the development of aviation in the USN.

Georgia's career was punctuated by an explosion in her after 205mm/8in turret, when black powder ignited, killing ten officers and men and injuring 11, but no permanent or lasting damage to the ship was caused and within a few weeks she was back in service. A veteran of the Great White Fleet, she made five trooping voyages from France. *Georgia* finished her service in the Pacific Fleet.

The remaining three ships of this class had similar careers: they became veterans of the Great White Fleet and were used as troopships post-war. *Nebraska* replaced *Alabama* in the fleet when it arrived at San Francisco in May 1908, and *New Jersey* was expended as a target. *Rhode Island* and her remaining sisters were sold for breaking up in 1923.

Virginia class

Class: *Virginia, Nebraska, Georgia, New Jersey, Rhode Island.* Launched 1904

Dimensions: Length – 134.5m/441ft 3in
Beam – 23.2m/76ft
Draught – 7.2m/23ft 9in

Displacement: 15,188 tonnes/14,948 tons

Armament: Main – 4 x 305mm/12in, 8 x 205mm/8in and 12 x 150mm/6in guns
Secondary – 12 x 75mm/3in, 12 x 3pdr guns and 4 x 535mm/21in torpedoes

Machinery: 12 Babcock & Wilcox boilers, 2 shafts,18,980kW/19,000ihp

Speed: 19 knots

Complement: 812 men

On commissioning *Virginia* and *Georgia* had 24 Niclausse boilers, later replaced by 24 Babcock & Wilcox.

Connecticut class

Connecticut and Louisiana extended the fashion in the USN pre-Dreadnoughts for multiple calibres of guns, which was mocked by Cuniberti. With so many guns of similar calibre, it was impossible to spot the fall of shot and so to range the guns: in part, the Dreadnought was a reaction to this design trend. Both ships took part in the Great White Fleet's circumnavigation, Connecticut as flagship.

Connecticut was also flagship of the USN Atlantic Fleet between 1907 and 1912. In the pre-war years, she visited the Mediterranean and the Caribbean on various policing and ceremonial duties and in 1913 protected American citizens and interests during disturbances in Mexico and Haiti. Like Louisiana, she was fitted as a troopship, making four voyages in 1919 to bring US soldiers back from France. In the 1920s, Connecticut served on the west coast before being sold for scrap in 1923.

Soon after entering service Louisiana sailed for Havana in response to an appeal by the Cuban president for American help in suppressing an insurrection. The new battleship carried a peace commission led by the US Secretary of War, William H. Taft, who arranged for a provisional government of the island, and Louisiana stood by while this was set up. Next Louisiana became the presidential yacht, taking President Theodore Roosevelt to inspect work on the construction of the Panama Canal and on a brief visit to Cuba.

Louisiana made an extensive visit to Europe in 1910 and 1911 but was soon back in the Caribbean to protect American lives and property during revolutionary disturbances in Mexico in 1913, during tension between the USA and Mexico in 1914 and again in 1915.

During World War I Louisiana was used for gunnery and engineering training and in late 1918 and early 1919 she made four voyages as a troop transport from Brest with returning US soldiers. She was sold for scrap in 1923.

Connecticut class	🇺🇸
Class: Connecticut, Louisiana. Launched 1904	
Dimensions: Length – 139 m/456ft 4in	
Beam – 23.4m/76ft 10in	
Draught – 7.46m/24ft 6in	
Displacement: 16,256 tonnes/16,000 tons	
Armament: Main – 4 x 305mm/12in, 8 x 205mm/8in and 12 x 180mm/7in guns.	
Secondary – 12 x 3pdr guns and 4 x 535mm/21in torpedoes	
Machinery: 12 boilers, 2 shafts,15,300kW/16,500ihp	
Speed: 18 knots	
Complement: 827 men	

ABOVE: **Connecticut at anchor in the Hudson river on the occasion of the fleet review of 1911. The launch in the foreground is typical of those carried in battleships.** LEFT: **Connecticut steaming at high speed, photographed by Enrique Muller in 1907.** BELOW: **President Roosevelt addresses the ship's company of Connecticut on the quarterdeck on return from their circumnavigation.**

LEFT: **A side-on view of one of the Vermont class. The mixed armament is distinctly pre-Dreadnought, while in Britain a revolution is taking place.** BELOW: **A detail of the bow decoration of *New Hampshire* taken while in dry dock. The picture shows the eagle figurehead, but unfortunately not the shape of the hull.**

Vermont class

American industry was beginning to show its muscle and the Vermont class of ships were repeats of the preceding Connecticut class of ships. Uniformity of build in a successful design was something which only the USN and the Royal Navy could be relied upon to achieve. All six ships were, however, made obsolescent by the Dreadnought revolution. *Vermont* was another of the Great White Fleet, which after her return to the USA joined the Atlantic Fleet. Her service alternated between European cruises and Caribbean deployments until 1914, when she landed a naval brigade (or battalion in USN usage) of 12 officers and 308 seamen and marines at Vera Cruz. The other ships that the USN sent to Mexico included the battleships *Vermont, Arkansas, New Hampshire, South Carolina* and *New Jersey*. There was only one American fatality in the shore fighting which ensued.

Like other pre-Dreadnought battleships *Vermont* was equipped as a troopship in the winter of 1918–19 and made four voyages from France with some 5,000 troops. She was scrapped in 1923.

Apart from the Great White Fleet, *Kansas*'s service was distinguished by making five crossings from Brest as a troopship. In 1920, she was visited by the Prince of Wales at Grassey Bay, Bermuda, and in November attended the inauguration of the new American governor of the German Samoa islands, ceded to the USA after World War I. Her name was struck from the Navy List on August 24, 1923, and she was sold for scrap in the same year.

Another member of the Great White Fleet, *Minnesota* led an unremarkable career until September 29, 1918, when she struck a mine, 32km/20 miles off Fenwick Island Shoal Lightship, which had apparently been laid by the German U-boat *U-117*. She was seriously damaged but suffered no loss of life. Repaired at Philadelphia, she was serviceable again by March 1919, when she brought 3,000 veterans from France. She was sold for scrap in 1924.

On her first deployment, *New Hampshire* carried a Marine Expeditionary Regiment to Colon, Panama, to protect and garrison Panama in 1908, and she attended the fleet review at New York that welcomed back the Great White Fleet. In 1916, *New*

Hampshire operated off Santo Domingo, where her captain had a hand in the newly installed government. In 1917 she was part of the convoy escort taking US troops to France, and in 1919 she made four voyages carrying them back again. *New Hampshire* was scrapped in 1923.

Vermont class

Class: *Vermont, Kansas, Minnesota, New Hampshire.* Launched 1905
Dimensions: Length – 139m/456ft 4in
 Beam – 23.4m/76ft 10in
 Draught – 7.6m/24ft 6in
Displacement: 16,256 tonnes/16,000 tons
Armament: Main – 4 x 305mm/12in,
 8 x 205mm/8in and 12 x 180mm/7in guns
 Secondary – 20 x 75mm/3in and
 12 x 3pdrs guns
Machinery: 12 boilers, 2 shafts,
 12,300kW/16,500ihp
Speed: 18 knots
Complement: 880 men
 The four ships of the Vermont class were repeats of the Connecticut class, with only minor differences in the secondary armament and complement.

Mississippi class

Mississippi and *Idaho* were the last of the USN's pre-Dreadnoughts, and were laid down and completed when Fisher's Dreadnought revolution had already made them obsolescent. Like other USN pre-Dreadnoughts, they carried a main battery of heavy, medium and small calibre guns. In a reaction to the rising cost of battleships the US Congress had limited their size, so that *Mississippi* and *Idaho* were actually smaller, slower and shorter-ranged than their predecessors.

Originally, both ships carried a single pole mast forward (known as a military mast) but soon after commissioning they were fitted with a cage or lattice mast aft, and in 1910 the forward pole mast was replaced by a second lattice mast, which balanced the design.

Neither ship saw battle: apart from deployments to the East Coast of North America and to the Caribbean, both made cruises to Europe. However, in June 1912, *Mississippi* landed US marines in Cuba to protect US interests, and carried men and equipment to Pensacola, Florida, to build a naval air station. In April and May 1914, she transported seaplanes and crews to Vera Cruz, Mexico, when an American squadron landed a force of 800 marines and seamen during a period of political unrest. *Mississippi*'s use as a seaplane tender was probably the first overseas deployment of aircraft by the USN. In 1909 *Mississippi* and in 1911 *Idaho* entered the Mississippi River for a tour of central US states with no seaboard. In 1910, both ships visited France and Britain, where they must have looked old-fashioned.

In July 1914, *Mississippi* and *Idaho* were sold to Greece, becoming the only USN battleships ever to be transferred to a foreign power. They were renamed *Lemnos* and *Kilkis* respectively and served in the Greek navy until April 1941 when they were sunk by German dive-bombers at Salamis, thus becoming the first American-built battleships to be lost to air attack.

Mississippi class

Class: *Mississippi, Idaho*. Launched 1905
Dimensions: Length – 116.4m/382ft
Beam – 23.5m/77ft
Draught – 7.5m/24ft 8in
Displacement: 13,210 tonnes/13,000 tons
Armament: Main – 4 x 305mm/12in,
8 x 205mm/8in and 8 x 180mm/7in guns
Secondary – 12 x 75mm/3in guns and
2 x 535mm/21in torpedoes
Machinery: 8 boilers, 2 shafts,
7,450kW/10,000ihp
Speed: 17 knots
Complement: 744 men

BOTTOM: *Mississippi* at anchor off Philadelphia in 1908 for Founders' Week. The ship's name, ready for illumination, is picked out in lights on the after superstructure. BELOW: Possibly the USN's first carrier air group. A squadron of Curtiss flying boats and floatplanes embarked in *Mississippi* during the Mexican crisis in 1914.

LEFT: *Yashima* and *Hatsuse* were built at the Armstrong Whitworth yard at Elswick. Here is *Hatsuse* at her launch on June 27, 1899. BELOW LEFT: *Fuji* and *Shikishima* were built at the Thames Iron Works on the Thames. Here is *Shikishima* at buoys in Malta, en route to Japan in 1900.

Fuji class

Class: *Fuji, Yashima.* Launched 1896
Dimensions: Length – 125.6m/412ft
  Beam – 22.5m/73ft 9in
  Draught – 8.1m/26ft 6in
Displacement: 12,518 tonnes/12,320 tons
Armament: Main – 4 x 305mm/12in,
  10 x 150mm/6in guns
  Secondary – 20 x 3pdr guns and
  5 x 455mm/18in torpedoes
Machinery: 14 boilers, 2 shafts.
  10,000kW/14,000ihp
Speed: 18 knots
Complement: 637 men

Fuji and Shikishima class

Building a navy was integral to Japan's rapid advance in the second half of the 19th century from feudal state to industrialized society. The first naval construction programme of home-built ships was influenced by the French *jeune école,* which advocated a fleet of cruisers and torpedo boats to counter battleships. However, the Sino-Japanese War of 1894–5 gave Japanese officers an appreciation of their navy's material and strategic necessities, and the Japanese, turning to Britain for battleships, came under the influence of the Royal Navy. Each ship of the 1896 expansion programme showed an improvement over the preceding one, although all six could be operated together.

The Imperial Japanese Navy began to build its strength in response to a perceived threat from the Chinese navy, which had acquired a number of modern German-built ships. The Chinese ships were armoured turret ships but the six ships that Japan bought in Britain were the new generation of pre-Dreadnoughts.

Fuji and *Yashima* were improved Royal Sovereigns, with weight being saved by placing most of the secondary armament behind shields rather than in armoured casemates. *Yashima*'s keel was cut away towards the bow, giving her a smaller turning circle than *Fuji*. The ships were refitted in 1901 when 12pdrs replaced the 3pdrs. Both ships took part in the Russo-Japanese war. *Yashima* was mined off Port Arthur on May 15, 1904, was taken in tow but capsized. *Fuji* fired the last shot at the Battle of Tsushima to sink the *Borodino*. *Fuji* was refitted in 1910 and reclassified as a coast defence ship. Disarmed under the Washington Treaty and used as a school ship, she capsized and was scrapped in 1945.

The two Shikishima class ships were improved British Majestics, and the armament was identical to the Fuji class. Both ships were at the bombardment of Port Arthur on February 9, 1904, and the subsequent blockade, where *Hatsuse* struck a mine on May 15, 1904. She was taken in tow by *Asahi* but struck a second mine whereupon her magazine exploded and she was lost. *Shikishima*, which was at the Battle of the Yellow Sea and the Battle of Tsushima, was classed as a coast defence ship in 1921, became a training ship in 1923 and was scrapped in 1947.

Shikishima class

Class: *Shikishima, Hatsuse.* Launched 1898–9
Dimensions: Length – 133.5m/438ft
  Beam – 23m/75ft 6in
  Draught – 8.4m/27ft 6in
Displacement: 15,088 tonnes/14,850 tons
Armament: Main – 4 x 305mm/12in and
  14 x 150mm/6in guns
  Secondary – 20 x 12pdr, 6/8 x 3pdr
  (6 x 1) guns and 5 x 455mm/18in torpedoes
Machinery: 25 Belleville boilers, 2 shafts.
  10,810kW/14,500ihp
Speed: 18 knots
Complement: 836 men (*Hatsuse* 741)

LEFT: *Asahi* at anchor in Portsmouth in
1900. Built by John Brown on the
Clyde, she was one of the last
Japanese ships to be built in Britain.
BELOW LEFT: *Asahi*'s sister ship *Mikasa*
underway. BELOW *Mikasa* still under
construction in the Vickers yard at
Barrow-in-Furness. The Japanese navy
had a strong preference for having
their ships built in Britain, and many
Japanese naval officers and naval
architects also studied in Britain at the
end of the 19th century and admired
what they found.

Mikasa and *Asahi*

*A*sahi was similar to the Shikishimas except she had two funnels instead of three. Mined on October 26, 1904, *Asahi* was repaired in time for the Battle of Tsushima. A gunnery training ship at the start of World War I, she was demilitarized after the Washington Naval Treaty, converted to a submarine salvage ship and torpedoed off Indo-China in 1942.

Mikasa was the last of six battleships ordered under the Japanese navy's ten-year programme of expansion. The 305mm/12in guns, which could be operated electrically or hydraulically and loaded at any angle of elevation or training, could fire at the rate of three shells every two minutes.

On February 8, 1904, *Mikasa* was Admiral Togo's flagship for a surprise attack on the Russian Far East Fleet at Port Arthur. When Admiral Vitgeft attempted a breakout to Vladivostok later in the year, he was defeated in the

Battle of the Yellow Sea. Vitgeft was killed when the battleship *Tsessarevitch* was hit by a 305mm/12in shell and the Russian fleet took refuge in Port Arthur. *Tsessarevitch* escaped to Tsingtao, where the Germans interned her, and by January 1905, when the Japanese took Port Arthur from the landward, the Russians had lost no less than seven battleships. Admiral Togo was hailed as the new Nelson.

When Admiral Rozhestvensky arrived in the Korea Strait after a 29,000km/ 18,000-mile journey from the Baltic, Togo's fleet was inferior to the Russian, but the Japanese possessed speed, morale and a tactical scheme. Togo in *Mikasa* out-gunned and outmanoeuvred the Russians, who by the end of the day had suffered six battleships and four others sunk, four captured, and three ships interned. *Mikasa* was hit 32 times but no Japanese ships were lost.

A magazine explosion killed 114 of *Mikasa*'s crew in September 1906, but she was refloated in the same year, and is preserved as a memorial.

Mikasa and *Asahi* ●

Class: *Asahi, Mikasa.* Launched 1899–1900
Dimensions: Length – 130m/426ft 6in
　　Beam – 22.9m/75ft 3in
　　Draught – 8.3m/27ft 3in
Displacement: 15,444 tonnes/15,200 tons
Armament: Main – 4 x 305mm/12in and
　　14 x 150mm/6in guns
　　Secondary – 20 x 12pdr, 6 x 3pdr guns and
　　4 x 455mm/18in torpedoes
Machinery: 25 boilers, 2 shafts.
　　11,930kW/15,000ihp
Speed: 18 knots
Complement: 836 men
There were minor differences in size between the two ships.

LEFT: **After a number of evolutionary types of warships, the German Brandenburg class is the first recognizable pre-Dreadnought. This is** *Wörth*, **photographed in 1900.** BELOW LEFT: *Brandenburg.* **Lost in the hamper amidships is a third, twin turret, which had to be of lesser calibre than the other main turrets in order to train to port or starboard.**

Brandenburg class

After a number of classes of German-built central battery ironclads and a class of coast defence battleships, the Brandenburgs marked the beginning of a fateful, and fatal, era of German naval expansion. Disparagingly the Royal Navy nicknamed these ships the "whalers". They were unusual in having a midships turret, whose barrels had to be shorter than the fore and aft turrets in order that they could be trained through the centre line to port or starboard. This could have given the Germans a lead in a Dreadnought-type arrangement of all centre-line guns, but the midships mounting, sited aft of the after funnel, caused blast damage and the idea was abandoned. Nevertheless, in a

further manifestation of growing German ambition, ships of this class saw service in China during the Boxer rebellion.

They were modernized in 1902 and 1904 with new boilers and the top-hamper was cut down. One torpedo tube was suppressed and an extra 105mm/4.13in fitted, but their secondary armament was regarded as weak by the standards of the time. They were also the first German warships to be fitted with radio.

In 1910, two ships of this class were sold to Turkey for nine million marks each, *Kurfürst Friedrich Wilhelm* as *Heireddin Barbarossa* and *Weissenburg*, which became the *Turgut Reis*. On August 8, 1915, *Heireddin Barbarossa*

was torpedoed and sunk with the loss of 253 lives by the British submarine *E11*, commanded by Lieutenant Commander Martin Nasmith, in the Dardanelles. *Turgut Reis* became a training ship in 1924 and was broken up 1938.

Brandenburg served overseas in 1900–1 to further German imperial ambitions, but when general war broke out in 1914 she was obsolete, and was relegated to coast defence duties in 1915. She became an accommodation ship at Libau in 1916–18, and was broken up at Danzig in 1920.

Wörth was categorized as a coastal defence ship in 1915 and then used as an accommodation ship at Danzig where she was broken up in 1919.

Brandenburg class

Class: *Brandenburg, Kurfürst Friedrich Wilhelm, Weissenburg, Wörth.* Launched 1891–2
Dimensions: Length – 115.7 m/379ft 7in
  Beam – 19.5m/64ft
  Draught – 7.9m/26ft
Displacement: 10,668 tonnes/10,500 tons
Armament: Main – 6 x 280mm/11in and
  6 x 105mm/4.13in guns
Secondary – 8 x 90mm/3.46in guns and
  6 x 450mm/17.7in torpedoes
Machinery: 12 boilers, 2-shaft TE,
  7,459kW/10,000ihp
Speed: 16 knots
Complement: 568 men

Kaiser class

N amed after German emperors past and present, these four ships carried a smaller main gun (approximately 240mm/9.4in) but a heavier secondary armament. Some of the 150mm/6in guns were mounted in turrets rather than casemates, and the triple shafts were typical German arrangements. However in other respects the Kaiser class still compared unfavourably with British designs.

Partly in response to the Dreadnought revolution, the Kaisers were reconstructed in 1907–10, with taller funnels, reduced superstructure and some rearrangement of the secondary and tertiary guns. *Kaiser Wilhelm II*, with her complement increased by 63, was fleet flagship until 1906. All ships of this class were disarmed and used as hulks in the war years. *Kaiser Wilhelm der Grosse* became a torpedo training ship, *Kaiser Wilhelm II*

became an HQ ship for the commander-in-chief, and the others became floating prisons. All were broken up in 1920 and 1921. The bow ornament of *Kaiser Freidrich III* is in a museum in Dresden.

LEFT: The Kaiser class were an incremental improvement over the Brandenburgs, but carried a smaller gun which just about qualified them as battleships.

Kaiser class

Class *Kaiser Freidrich III, Kaiser Wilhelm II, Kaiser Wilhelm der Grosse, Kaiser Barbarossa,* Launched 1896–1900
Dimensions: Length – 125.3m/411ft
  Beam 20.4m/67ft,
  Draught 8.25m/27ft
Displacement: 11,920 tonnes/11,599 tons
Armament: Main – 4 x 240mm/9.4in, 18 x 150mm/6in guns
  Secondary – 12 x 88mm/3.46in guns and 6 x 450mm/17.7in torpedoes
Machinery: 12 boilers, 3 shafts. 10,440kW/14,000ihp
Speed: 17 knots
Complement: 651

Wittelsbach class

T he Wittelsbach class were improved Kaisers, although the improvements were not great: they carried a similar armament and somewhat extended armour. By World War I they were too slow and vulnerable to stand in the line of battle, and were used for training. By 1916 all ships of this class had been

disarmed, so when Germany signed away the High Sea Fleet in the Armistice of 1918, she was allowed to keep these obsolete ships. *Mecklenburg* became a floating prison, and was scrapped in 1921. Converted towards the end of World War I to depot ships for minesweeping motor launches,

Schwaben and *Wittelsbach* each carried 12 shallow-draught minesweepers, but they too were scrapped in 1921–2. *Zähringen* became a target ship in 1917, and in 1926 was converted so she could be radio-controlled. She was sunk by the British Royal Air Force bombing at Gotenhafen (Gdynia) in 1944.

LEFT: The Wittelsbachs were slightly larger and improved Kaisers, with the same gun. Unlike the British pre-Dreadnoughts which could be sent to overseas stations, there was nowhere for these ships to go and they were disarmed by the Germans in 1916.

Wittelsbach class

Class: *Wittelsbach, Wettin, Zähringen, Schwaben, Mecklenburg.* Launched 1900–1
Dimensions: Length – 126.8m/416ft
  Beam – 22.8m/74ft 9in
  Draught – 8m/26ft 4in
Displacement: 12,798 tonnes/12,596 tons
Armament: Main – 4 x 240mm/9.4in and 18 x 150mm/6in guns
  Secondary – 12 x 88mm/3.46in guns and 6 x 450mm/17.7in torpedoes
Machinery: 12 boilers, 3 shafts, 11,180kW/15,000ihp
Speed: 17 knots
Complement: 683 men

LEFT: *Preussen* underway at speed. The large bow wave seems to be characteristic, indicating perhaps that German naval architects did not quite understand their subject. BELOW: *Hessen* passing through the Kiel Canal, probably in the interwar years. The Braunschweig class were among the small number of ships that the Germans were allowed to keep under the terms of the armistice.

Braunschweig class

The Braunschweigs marked a stepped improvement over the previous two classes of German pre-Dreadnoughts. The forward main gun was mounted on the forecastle instead of one deck above with a battery of lesser guns beneath. The guns were heavier (280mm/11in as opposed to 240mm/9.4in) and the armour was slightly thicker. Although 1,524 tonnes/1,500 tons larger, with extra boilers and three funnels, they produced a speed of 8 knots, which was one knot faster than the Wittelsbachs and Kaisers. However, the 280mm/11in guns were still lighter than the standard British 305mm/12in, and while they were being completed between 1904 and 1906, they were overtaken by the Dreadnought revolution. In the early part of World War I they were stationed in the Baltic, but between 1916 and 1918 they were disarmed.

Preussen and *Lothringen* were converted to depot ships for minesweeping motor boats in 1919 and broken up in 1931. One midships section of the hull of *Preussen* survived as a torpedo target and for explosive trials. Renamed *Vierkant* (meaning "even keel"), she was sunk by bombing in 1944 and not raised and broken up until 1954.

Braunschweig, *Elsass* and *Hessen* were rebuilt as coast defence ships in the 1920s, with much of their original armament, but were sold for breaking up between 1931 and 1935.

Hessen survived as a radio-controlled target ship and was then taken over by the Soviet Union in 1946 and given the name *Tsel*.

Braunschweig class

Class: *Braunschweig, Elsass, Hessen, Preussen, Lothringen.* Launched 1902–4

Dimensions: Length – 127.7m/419ft
Beam – 25.6m/84ft
Draught – 8.1m/26ft 7in

Displacement: 14,394 tonnes/14,167 tons

Armament: Main – 4 x 280mm/11in and
14 x 170mm/6.7in guns
Secondary – 18 x 88mm/3.46in guns,
4 x machine-guns and 6 x 450mm/17.7in
torpedoes

Machinery: 14 boilers, 3-shaft TE,
12,677kW/17,000ihp

Speed: 18 knots

Complement: 743 men

LEFT: **Deutschland was the name of the last class of German pre-Dreadnoughts. Here one is seen passing eastbound along the Kiel Canal. Despite their obsolescence they took part in the Battle of Jutland.** BELOW: **A battleship of the Kaiser class firing a broadside to starboard.** BOTTOM: **Paint ship! A task familiar to sailors old and new in every navy. This essential work is not just for smartness but also keeps the hull well-maintained and rust-free.**

Deutschland class

The Deutschlands were the last pre-Dreadnoughts of the Imperial German Navy. They were similar to the Braunschweigs, but had slightly differently shaped funnels and thicker armour. The two twin turrets and the mixed secondary and tertiary armament marked the epitome of the pre-Dreadnoughts. Ordered and laid down amid rumours, and then hard news, of Fisher's Dreadnought revolution, all five ships of the class were completed at great expense while Germany considered its options of how to react to developments in Britain.

Although obsolescent, the Deutschlands took part in the Battle of Jutland in 1916, where concern for their vulnerability and slowness may have influenced Scheer's tactics. The weakness in the protection and magazine arrangements of the secondary armament was reckoned to have caused the loss of *Pommern* when a single torpedo, fired by a British destroyer, hit her and she blew up.

By 1917 all ships of the class had been removed from the line of battle. *Deutschland* was disarmed and broken up in 1920, but the three others survived into World War II. *Schlesien* and *Schleswig-Holstein* were refitted in the 1920s and rebuilt about 1930, when the fore-funnel was trunked into the midships one. Better anti-aircraft (AA) armament was fitted, and in World War II numerous 40mm/1.57in and other light AA guns were added as well.

After World War I, *Schleswig-Holstein* became an accommodation ship and then in 1926 flagship of the Kreigsmarine. Afterwards she became a

training ship for the newly resurgent Reichsmarine, but she was bombed and sunk in 1944.

Schlesien became an accommodation ship at the end of World War I, was refitted in the 1920s, and mined off Swinemunde in 1944.

Deutschland class

Class: *Deutschland, Hannover, Pommern, Schlesien, Schleswig-Holstein.* Launched 1904–6
Dimensions: Length – 127.6m/418ft 8in
  Beam – 22.3m/73ft
  Draught – 8.2m/27ft
Displacement: 14,218 tonnes/13,993 tons
Armament: Main – 4 x 280mm/11in and
  14 x 170mm/6.7in guns
  Secondary – 20 x 88mm/3.46in guns and
  6 x 450mm/17.7in torpedoes
Machinery: 12 boilers, 3 shafts,
  11,930kW/16,000ihp
Speed: 18 knots

LEFT: **French designers produced several high-sided ships with massive superstructures during the 1890s, such as the *Brennus*.**

Brennus

Class: *Brennus*. Launched 1891
Dimensions: Length – 110.3m/361ft 10in
　Beam – 20.4m/66ft 11in
　Draught – 8.3m/27ft 2in
Displacement: 11,370 tonnes/11,190 tons
Armament: Main – 3 x 340mm/13.5in and
　10 x 160mm/6.4in guns
　Secondary – 4 x 9pdr and 14 x 3pdr guns
　4 x 455mm/18in torpedoes
Machinery: 32 Belleville boilers, 2 shafts,
　12,304kW/16,900ihp
Speed: 18 knots
Complement: 673 men

Brennus turret ship

The French built a number of turret ships of which *Brennus* was the last. Her designers tried to cram in too much and her masts and superstructure had to be reduced before she was considered safe. She was heavily armoured with a belt 255mm/10in to 455mm/18in thick, which extended upwards to cover her upper deck and the barbettes. She carried her three, long 340mm/13.4in guns in single and twin barbettes, and,

also unusual for her time, had no ram: this and her high freeboard qualified *Brennus* as the first true ocean-going battleship of the modern age.

In the previous ten years France had built ten mastless turret ships, but the centre-line armoured pivot turrets qualified *Brennus* as the first modern battleship. She was also protected with face-hardened armour made by the Harvey process invented in the USA.

Like many of her predecessors she was overweight and unstable. At just 5 degrees of heel her armoured belt was submerged and hydraulic power to the guns was interrupted, so both the superstructure and the military mainmast had to be reduced.

Charles Martel class

The French built five similar ships, sometimes considered as one class: *Charles Martel*, *Carnot*, *Jauréguiberry*, *Masséna* and *Bouvet*. *Charles Martel* had a high freeboard forward, a flying bridge between her funnels and was cut down aft. *Carnot* had a reduced superstructure, no flying deck or military mainmast, and her funnels were further apart. *Jauréguiberry* had a shorter hull which brought the guns close to the ends of the

ship, and, in the earlier days of water-tube boilers (needing numerous tight joints), she suffered a boiler explosion. *Masséna* was similar in appearance to *Charles Martel*, and *Bouvet*, generally regarded as the best of these ships, differed in the hull not being cut down and in having two short military masts.

The armament was generally similar: three 305mm/12in guns on the centre-line and two 275mm/10.8in guns

mounted midships on the tumblehome, and six 140mm/5.5in and numerous smaller quick-firing guns that varied throughout the class. These ships also had numerous small compartments, called the *tranche cellulaire*, which could be filled with coal or stores and were intended to limit the effects of damage.

Charles Martel class

Class: *Charles Martel, Carnot, Jauréguiberry,*
　Masséna, Bouvet. Launched 1893–6
Dimensions: Length – 115.5m/378ft 11in
　Beam – 21.6m/71ft
　Draught – 8.4m/27ft 6in
Displacement: 11,881 tonnes/11,693 tons
Armament: Main – 2 x 305mm/12in,
　2 x 275mm/10.8in and 6 x 140mm/5.5in guns
　Secondary – 4 x 9pdr, 12–18 x 3pdr guns and
　2 x 455mm/18in torpedoes
Machinery: 24 Lagrafel d'Allest boilers, 2 shafts,
　10,910kW/14,200 to 12,304kW/16,900ihp
Speed: 18 knots
Complement: 644 men

LEFT: **The five ships of the Charles Martel class were meant to be one class, but as a result of being built in different yards by different designers, individual ships varied.**

Charlemagne class

These were the first French battleships armed with two twin mountings, as was usual in other navies, and the first to have three shafts. Less beamy and lighter in displacement than the Charles Martel class, most observers reckoned they were too small.

It was recognized that early French designs were vulnerable to hull damage, so in the Charlemagne class the belt was extended from 1.5m/5ft below to 45.5cm/18in above the waterline, and in its midships portion it was 355mm/14in thick, tapering to 205mm/8in at the lower edge and 255mm/10in at the extremities. Inboard there was the usual French arrangement of a cofferdam and cellular compartments.

The main 305mm/12in guns were mounted in pivot turrets fore and aft, the 140mm/5.5in guns in a battery at the upper deck level (and two at forecastle deck level) and the tertiary 100mm/4in guns in the superstructure. All the Charlemagne class took part in World War I.

On March 18, 1915, *Gaulois* was engaged and hit by Turkish shore batteries and a single shell hit her port bow below the waterline, tearing off the hull plating. Flooding spread via the ventilation trunking and she had to be beached on Rabbit Island, north of Tenedos. After being refloated she went to Malta for repairs. However, on December 27, 1916, *Gaulois* was on passage from the French base at Corfu to Salonika when the German submarine *UB-47* eluded her escort and torpedoed her: she floated for 25 minutes, sufficient time for most of her crew to be rescued, before settling on an even keel.

Charlemagne was also in the bombardment groups but escaped serious damage, and survived the war to be stricken in 1920.

St Louis served seemingly without distinction or notoriety until she was scrapped in 1933.

TOP: **The French ships looked so big because they were compact. The Charlemagne class were smaller in displacement than their predecessors but more heavily armed.** ABOVE: **Like the British pre-Dreadnoughts, these French ships were relegated to secondary theatres of warfare. *Gaulois* was sunk off the Dardanelles, re-floated and sunk again.**

Charlemagne class

Class: *Charlemagne, St Louis, Gaulois.*
Launched 1896
Dimensions: Length – 114m/374ft in
  Beam – 20.2m/66ft 5in
  Draught – 8.4m/27ft 6in
Displacement: 11,278 tonnes/11,100 tons
Armament: Main – 4 x 305mm/12in,
  10 x 140mm/5.5in, and 8 x 100mm/4in guns
  Secondary – 20 x 3pdr guns and
  2 x 455mm/18in torpedoes
Machinery: 20 Belleville boilers, 3-shafts VTE,
  10,810kW/14,500iph
Speed: 18 knots
Complement: 694 men

Iéna class

In general design *Iéna* was an enlarged *Charlemagne* with a complete armoured belt extended above and below the waterline 325mm/12.8in thick amidships and tapering to 230mm/9in at the ends, and there was the usual, French, cellular layer below the armoured deck. The 305mm/12in guns were arranged with the 160mm/6.4in in casemates on the main deck, and the four amidships guns in sponsons over the pronounced tumblehome. Despite being fitted with bilge keels, *Iéna* was known to roll and pitch uncomfortably.

Iéna was one of a list of ships that suffered a spontaneous explosion. The magazine cooling gear had been removed while she was in dry-dock in Toulon, when decomposing nitrocellulose propellant ignited and set light to the after 305mm/12in magazine. The whole after part of the ship was wrecked and the midships section badly damaged, and she was afterwards used as a target.

Suffren, which took four years to complete, differed in that four of her 160mm/6.4in guns were placed in turrets on the upper deck and the rest in casemates. She was hit during the main attack on the Dardanelles on March 18, 1915, when three casemate guns were put out of action and an ammunition fire started. She was reputed to have been saved from explosion because the charges were in metal cases. However, on November 26, 1916, while on her way to refit at Lorient, *Suffren* was torpedoed and sunk by the German submarine *U-52* off the Portuguese coast. There were no survivors.

Henri IV was an experimental ship, not completed until 1903. She had only 1.22m/4ft freeboard over most of her length, except forward where it was built up to normal deck height, and there was the usual cellular layer inboard of the torpedo bulkhead. She had one of the first superfiring turrets, though the blast effects were said to be severe as the muzzle of the 140mm/5.5in gun barrel was too short even to clear the sighting hood of the 275mm/10.8in gun below it. *Henri IV* saw service at Gallipoli, survived World War I and was scrapped in 1921.

LEFT, BELOW LEFT AND BOTTOM: The three ships seen here, *Suffren* (left) and *Henri IV* (below left) and *Iéna* (bottom), were singletons, built at a time of great change in French design. It was symptomatic that *Henri IV* spent over six years from being laid down to completion.

Iéna class

Class: *Suffren.* Launched 1899
Dimensions: Length – 125.5m/411ft 9in
    Beam – 21.4m/70ft 2in
    Draught – 8.4m/27ft 6in
Displacement: 12,728 tonnes/12,527 tons
Armament: Main – 4 x 305mm/12in, 10 x
    160mm/6.4in and 8 x 100mm/4in guns
    Secondary – 22 x 3pdr guns and
    2 x 455mm/18in torpedoes
Machinery: 24 Niclausse boilers, 3 shafts,
    12,453kW/16,700ihp
Speed: 17.9 knots
Complement: 714 men

Class: *Iéna.* Launched 1898
Dimensions: Length – 122.2m/400ft 9in
Beam – 20.8m/68ft 3in
Draught – 8.4m/27ft 6in
Displacement: 12,050 tonnes/11,860 tons
Armament: Main – 4 x 305mm/12in,
    8 x 160mm/6.4in and 8 x 100mm/4in guns
    Secondary - 20 x 3pdr guns and
    2 x 455mm/18in torpedoes
Machinery: 20 Belleville boilers, 3 shafts,
    12,304kW/16,500ihp
Speed: 18 knots
Complement: 682 men

Class: *Henri IV.* Launched 1899
Dimensions: Length – 108m/354ft 4in
    Beam – 22.2m/72ft 10in
    Draught – 7m/22ft 11in
Displacement: 8,948 tonnes/8,807 tons
Armament: Main – 2 x 275mm/10.8in,
    7 x 140mm/5.5in guns
    Secondary – 12 x 3pdr guns and
    2 x 455mm/18in torpedoes
Machinery: 12 Niclausse boilers, 3 shafts,
    8,575kW/11,500ihp
Speed: 17 knots
Complement: 464 men

LEFT: **At last the French navy was prepared to build big. *République* and her sister ship *Patrie* were an adequate size, although their design when completed in 1906–8 was obsolescent.**

République class

Class: *République, Patrie.* Launched 1902–3
Dimensions: Length – 133.8m/439ft
  Beam – 24.3m/79ft 7in
  Draught – 8.4m/27ft 7in
Displacement: 14,839 tonnes/14,605 tons
Armament: Main – 4 x 305mm/12in and
  18 x 160mm/6.4in guns
  Secondary – 25 x 3pdr guns and
  2 x 455mm/18in torpedoes
Machinery: 24 Niclausse boilers, 3 shafts,
  13,423kW/18,000ihp
Speed: 19 knots
Complement: 766 men

République class

Previous French designs of pre-Dreadnought battleships had been poor compromises between armament and armour, but in *République* and her sister ships they were at last able to solve their design problem. However, this class took so long to build they were not completed until 1906 and 1908, when Fisher's revolution was well under way.

In appearance, they owed something to the experimental *Henri IV*, with a high forecastle that ran back to the mainmast. Their three funnels, two forward and one well separated aft, and a tall pole mainmast gave them a distinctive appearance. In addition to the armoured belt and decks the cellular construction that the French preferred consisted of a short cofferdam, a passageway and coal bunkers, before reaching a central passageway. The main guns were placed high in the ship and there were six twin-turreted 160mm/6.4in guns at the forecastle deck level. Both vessels saw out World War I in the Mediterranean, when *Patrie*'s casemate 160mm/6.4in guns were mounted ashore in Salonica. Both were stricken in the 1920s.

Liberté class

The *Liberté* was very similar to the *République*, the main difference being the secondary armament of ten 190mm/7.6in guns, arranged six in single turrets at forecastle deck level, and two in casemates forward at upper deck and aft at main deck levels.

The armour was similar to the *République*, but following the French practice of farming out construction to different yards all three ships differed slightly in their displacement and draught. The Liberté class also had improved anti-torpedo 9pdr and 3pdr guns, similar to those later fitted in *République*.

Liberté blew up in Toulon harbour in 1911, the cause again being spontaneous ignition of decomposing nitrocellulose propellant, this time in one of the forward 190mm/7.6in magazines. The flooding arrangements were found to be inadequate and the resulting fire and explosion affected all the fore part of the ship. She was a total loss, although the wreck was not raised and scrapped until 1925.

The other three ships stayed in the Mediterranean during World War I and were stricken in the early 1920s.

Liberté class

Class: *Democratie, Justice, Liberté, Verite.*
  Launched 1904–7
Dimensions: Length – 133.8m/439ft in
  Beam – 24.3m/79ft 7in
  Draught – 8.35m/27ft 5in
Displacement: 14,722 tonnes/14,489 tons
Armament: Main – 4 x 305mm/12in and
  10 x 190mm/7.6in guns
  Secondary – 13 x 9pdr, 10 x 3pdr guns and
  2 x 455mm/18in torpedoes
Machinery: 22 Belleville boilers, 3 shafts,
  13,795kW/18,500ihp.
  Justice had 24 Niclausse boilers.
Speed: 19 knots
Complement: 739 men

LEFT: **The French were now also building ships in batches, but still farming out individual units to separate yards. *Liberté* is therefore typical of her class but there were minor differences between individual ships.**

Danton class

After the 1904 Anglo-French Entente Cordiale, the French navy agreed to concentrate in the Mediterranean, and the Premier Armée Navale consisted of 21 battleships, including four newly commissioned Dreadnoughts and the six Danton class semi-Dreadnoughts. First, the French fleet escorted troop transports from North Africa and by the end of August 1914, 14 French battleships were based at Malta to forestall a breakout from the Adriatic by the Austro-Hungarian fleet. In September they bombarded Cattaro and Lissa, and two pre-Dreadnoughts joined the British squadron watching the Dardanelles to prevent the battlecruiser *Goeben* from breaking out.

Once Italy entered the war in May 1915, the French fleet moved to bases at Brindisi and Corfu. In the winter of 1915/6 the French evacuated the defeated Serbian army from Albania to Salonika, and in spring 1916 took an active part in the Dardanelles campaign. The pre-Dreadnoughts *Gaulois, Bouvet, Charlemagne* and *Suffren* were badly damaged when hidden Turkish guns came into action during the landings on March 18, 1915, and they ran into a minefield. *Bouvet* was sunk.

In December 1916, French warships forced the pro-German Greek government to support Allied policies, landing sailors in Athens, briefly bombarding the city and seizing Greek warships. Later in the war the French navy concentrated its efforts more on anti-submarine warfare and convoy protection, but in 1918 formed part of the Aegean Sea Squadron deployed to prevent a breakout from the Dardanelles by the Turks.

TOP: **By their date these ships are Dreadnoughts, but they incorporated many pre-Dreadnought features, such as a large calibre secondary armament mounted to port and starboard.** ABOVE: **The Dantons were impressive high-sided ships.** *Danton* **is seen here with her three portside twin 9-in guns trained out.**

The Danton class ships were the first large turbine-engine ships. Compared to République and Liberté class they were another 3,048 tonnes/3,000 tons bigger, the extra displacement being used for a heavier secondary armament rather than speed. Their large batteries of rapid-fire tertiary guns made them useful in the confined waters of the Mediterranean.

The ships fitted with Belleville boilers made slightly more than 20 knots on trials, while the others were a knot slower. During World War I all ships received additional 75mm/3in anti-aircraft guns, and *Condorcet, Vergniaud* and *Voltaire* had their

Danton class

Class: *Danton, Voltaire, Condorcet, Diderot, Mirabeau, Vergniaud.* Launched 1909–10

Dimensions: Length – 144.9m/475ft 5in
　　　　　　Beam – 25.8m/84ft 8in
　　　　　　Draught – 9.2m/30ft 2in

Displacement: 18,612 tonnes/18,318 tons

Armament: Main – 4 x 305mm/12in,
　　　　　　12 x 240mm/9.4in guns
　　　　　　Secondary – 16 x 75mm/2.95in,
　　　　　　10 x 45mm/1.77in guns and
　　　　　　2 x 455mm/18in torpedoes

Machinery: 26 Belleville boilers, 4 shafts (Parsons
　　　　　　turbines), 16,778kW/22,500shp

Speed: 19.2 knots

Complement: 681 men

TOP: **This stern view shows how similar in size the main and secondary armaments were.** ABOVE: **The layout of the funnel made for easy recognition of the class.** BELOW: **Their appearance changed little during World War I.**

mainmasts shortened in 1918 so they could carry kite balloons. In 1918, the main guns had their range increased from 13,700m/14,983yd to 18,000m/19,690yd and the class were given a fire control system like other Dreadnoughts. All except *Danton* and *Diderot* were off to Athens in December 1916 when *Mirabeau* fired four rounds over the city as part of a pro-Allied demonstration, one of which landed near the Royal Palace.

Danton was zigzagging south-west of Sicily en route to the Allied blockade lines in the Straits of Otranto when, on March 19, 1917, the German submarine *U-64* torpedoed her. *Danton* was carrying drafts to the fleet greatly in excess of her own crew but fortunately she took some 45 minutes to sink and 296 men were saved. However, 806 men were lost, making this the worst disaster of the war at sea for the French navy.

Voltaire was also off Athens in December 1916 with four of her sisters, and in the Aegean in 1918. On the night of October 10/11, 1918, near Antikythira, she was twice torpedoed by the German *UB-48* but survived with little damage. On November 13, 1918, she was part of the Allied fleet which anchored off Constantinople.

Vergniaud and *Mirabeau* entered the Black Sea to operate off the Crimea against the Red Army. There *Mirabeau* ran aground in a snowstorm on February 13, 1919, and was salvaged in April 1919 only after the forward part of the ship including the main gun had been dismantled. She was used for trials and then stricken in 1921, though she and *Vergniaud* continued to be used for explosives experiments afterwards.

Condorcet, Diderot and *Voltaire* were modernized in the 1920s and fitted with improved underwater protection, but from 1927 onwards they served as training ships, and *Diderot* and *Voltaire* were stricken in the 1930s.

Condorcet became a depot ship at Toulon, where on November 27, 1942, an attempt to blow her up by loyal French officers was botched and she was taken over by the German navy as a barrack ship. In August 1944, she was bombed by an Allied aircraft and sunk only to be re-floated in September 1944. She was sold and broken up in 1945.

LEFT: **Italian naval architects were not burdened with a huge legacy of previous draughtsmanship. Starting from first principles they produced a balanced design like** *Italia*. BELOW: **A sister ship to** *Italia*, *Lepanto* **had four instead of six funnels in the same balanced layout.** *Italia* **was later remodelled into the same funnel configuration. These two ships, which were much admired by Fisher, were for some time the largest and fastest in the world, and might be regarded as the forerunner to the battlecruiser type.**

Italia class

The Italian navy recovered slowly from the disaster of the Battle of Lissa in 1866, but built some fine ships. Italian naval architects were talented and open to new ideas, while the navy concentrated on quality rather than quantity, and so in the pre-Dreadnought era was able to rival the British and French navies in the Mediterranean. The turret ships *Duilio* and *Dandolo* when laid down in 1873 were faster at 15 knots and more heavily armed with 450mm/17.7in muzzle-loaders than any other battleship. Although ugly ships, they were admired by Jacky Fisher, then in command of the Royal Navy's largest warship, *Inflexible*.

In the 1870s, the Italian engineer Benedetto Brin designed two ships, *Italia* and *Lepanto*, which in many ways were the forerunners of the battlecruiser. Different sources describe these ships as large, fast battleships or strategic cruisers. The 430mm/17in guns were at the limits of gun technology, and Brin dispensed with side armour, building the hulls of iron and steel and covering the sides with wood and zinc. Although they each took some nine years to complete and were relatively weakly armoured, these two ships were for many years in the 1880s the largest and fastest in the world. Each was also capable of embarking a division of infantry.

Italia as built had six funnels, three forward and three aft, but was rebuilt in 1905–8 to look like *Lepanto* with just four funnels. The guns were sited in pairs amidships around a central control tower and an elegant military mast. They were later fitted with more quick-firing guns and two additional torpedo tubes. The single pole mast was also replaced and two shorter ones were fitted. Neither, however, saw any action.

Lepanto was stricken in 1914 and then *Italia* in 1921, after a career as a floating battery, a cereal carrier and a depot ship.

Italia class

Class: *Italia, Lepanto.* Launched 1880–3
Dimensions: Length – 122m/400ft 3in
    Beam – 22.5m/73ft 11in
    Draught – 8.7m/28ft 8in
Displacement: 13,897 tonnes/13,678 tons
Armament: Main – 4 x 430mm/17in and
    7 x 150mm/5.9in guns
Secondary – 4 x 120mm/4.7in guns and
    4 x 355mm/14in torpedoes
Machinery: 24 boiler, 4 shafts, 8,389kW/11,250ihp
Speed: 18 knots
Complement: 669 men

Ruggiero di Lauria class

On March 8, 1880, one of *Duilio's* huge muzzle-loading guns was double-charged in a drill error and blew up. The accident prejudiced the Italian public against large ships and large guns, which members of the government opposed already on the grounds of cost.

The task of designing a successor ship to the Italia class was given to an engineer called Giuseppe Micheli and for once Italian ingenuity failed. Micheli tried various ideas but could only come up with an improved *Duilio* type. The improvements included a forecastle, which the original design had lacked; placing the breech-loading guns in barbettes and better armour, but the class was already obsolete when they were completed in 1888–91.

Francesco Morisini was used as a target and sunk in 1909; her guns were mounted on an Italian monitor used to provide the army with gunfire support. The other two were stricken in 1911. *Andrea Doria* became a floating battery in World War I and was broken up in 1929, but *Ruggiero di Lauria* survived until 1943 as an oil bunker at La Spezia, and was not broken up until 1946.

BELOW LEFT: **The low freeboard of the Ruggiero de Lauria class harked back to former designs and may have only been suitable for the relatively calm waters of the Adriatic.** BELOW RIGHT: **A rare picture of an Italian warship being built on stocks. Given the lack of tide in the Mediterranean and Adriatic it scarcely seems possible that she will reach the sea.** BOTTOM: **Despite their unusual appearance, the Ruggiero di Lauria class were heavily armed ships carrying 430mm/17in guns.**

Ruggiero di Lauria class

Class: *Ruggiero di Lauria, Francesco Morosini, Andrea Doria.* Launched 1884–5
Dimensions: Length – 100m/328ft 1in
Beam – 19.8m/65ft 1in
Draught – 8.3m/27ft 2in
Displacement: 10,045 tonnes/9,886 tons
Armament: Main – 4 x 430mm/17in and
2 x 150mm/6in guns
Secondary – 4 x 120mm/4.7in guns and
2 x 355mm/14in torpedoes
Machinery: 8 boilers, 2 shafts, 7,898kW/10,591ihp
Speed: 16 knots
Complement: 507 men

LEFT: **This photograph shows the 120mm/4.7in guns run out and trained to starboard as they might be when repelling a torpedo-boat attack.**

ABOVE: **Seen in profile the twin side-by-side funnels merge into one and** *Re Umberto*, **seen here, looks like any other pre-Dreadnought.** BELOW: **Freeboard and its consequent seaworthiness did not impinge much upon Italy's considerations of design, but her architects were open to novel ideas such as single and twin funnels.**

Re Umberto class

Benedetto Brin (1833–98) worked until the age of 40 as a naval engineer. In 1873, the Italian navy minister, Simone Pacoret di Saint Bon, made Brin undersecretary of state, and the two men complemented each other; di Saint Bon had the ideas and Brin accomplished them in his designs for Italian warships. When Brin himself became the navy minister, he developed di Saint Bon's ideas and is credited with creating the first organic scheme for the development of the Italian fleet. He had already designed the turret ships *Duilio* and *Dandolo* and Italy's first battleships, the Italia class, when he temporarily abandoned big ship designs in favour of smaller warships.

The Italian warship-building industry was insignificant when Brin took office, but under his guidance it made rapid progress. During his time, he helped create private shipyards and machine shops, and introduced the indigenous manufacture of armour, steel plates and guns. Brin's appointment as minister for foreign affairs in 1892 was probably an over-promotion, but his previous achievements qualify him as the creator of the Italian navy.

Two ships were ordered in 1883, and when Brin became navy minister for the second time he decided to build a third ship of the same class. The layout showed Brin's hand: a tall central mast, and a symmetrical disposition of the funnels and turrets fore and aft. The forward funnels were, however, a pair that sat abreast of each other. In Brin's design he continued to sacrifice armour for speed and armament, and the armoured belt of the Re Umberto class was only 100mm/4in thick. These ships, like many Italian and French ships of the period, were a long time in building and when they were complete, they rapidly became obsolete. Nevertheless all three ships survived World War I.

Re Umberto was laid up in 1912 but was later used as a depot ship and as a floating battery. When the Italian navy planned to force the Austro-Hungarian port of Pola, she was fitted as an assault ship, stripped of her former armament in favour of 75mm/3in guns and trench mortars. The idea was that she should

rush the harbour followed by a flotilla of small craft, but the war ended before this scheme could be put into effect. *Sicilia* became a repair ship and *Sardegna* a depot ship. All three were stricken in the 1920s.

Re Umberto class

Class: *Re Umberto, Sicilia, Sardegna.* Launched 1888–91

Dimensions: Length – 122m/400ft 3in
Beam – 23.4m/76ft 10in
Draught – 9.3m/30ft 6in

Displacement: 13,892 tonnes/13,673 tons

Armament: Main – 4 x 340mm/13.5in and
16 x 120mm/4.7in guns
Secondary – 16 x 6pdr, 10 x 37mm/1.46in guns
and 5 x 450mm/17.7in torpedoes

Machinery: 18 boilers, 2 shafts,
11,180kW/15,000ihp

Speed: 20 knots

Complement: 733 men

Ammiraglio di Saint Bon class

Italian strategists had not fixed on the size or type of ship they wanted, so for their next class of ship they were driven by the government, which wanted ships to be as small and as cheap as possible. So when di Saint Bon died, Brin returned temporarily and he proposed a medium-sized ship with relatively small 255mm/10in guns. The design showed the symmetry of earlier Italian ships and followed the style that the British had started with *Collingwood* and Brin had copied with *Re Umberto*: two twin guns forward and two aft. The ships took some eight years to complete, but not even Brin could not save the design from its inherent weaknesses: the ships were too slow at 18 knots and small, and their freeboard was only 2.7m/9ft. Overall they were too weak to

ABOVE: **Italian naval architects were beginning to be influenced by overseas developments, but** *Ammiraglio di Saint Bon* **still has the unusual arrangement of a single, central mast.** BELOW LEFT: *Emanuel Filiberto* **at the end of World War I.**

stand in the line of battle and too slow to catch even a cruiser. They saw limited service in World War I and were not broken up until 1920.

Ammiraglio di Saint Bon class	
Class: *Ammiraglio di Saint Bon, Emanuel Filiberto.* Launched 1897	
Dimensions: Length – 105m/344ft 6in	
Beam – 21.1m/69ft 3in	
Draught – 7.7m/25ft 2in	
Displacement: 10,244 tonnes/10,082 tons	
Armament: Main – 4 x 255mm/10in and	
8 x 150mm/6in guns	
Secondary – 8 x 55mm/2.24in guns and	
4 x 450mm/17.7in torpedoes	
Machinery: 12 boilers, 2 shafts,	
10,664kW/14,300ihp	
Speed: 18 knots	
Complement: 557/567 men	

Regina Margherita class

The Italian navy wanted a ship to match the Austro-Hungarian Habsburg class, and so Brin's last effort was the Regina Margherita class. These were intended to be modern, fast and well-armed ships, even at the expense of armoured protection, as in so many Italian designs. With this class the Italians reverted to a larger battleship design although the result was smaller than other contemporary, foreign battleships. Symmetry was carried to an extreme with two funnels amidships, fore and aft, two matching pole masts, and forward and after combined control towers and bridges. Unlike their

immediate predecessors the Ammiraglio di Saint Bon class, which could burn coal or oil, these ships could only use coal. Brin died while the class was under construction and the second ship was named after him.

On September 27, 1915, while in Brindisi harbour, *Benedetto Brin* suffered a fire and exploded killing 450 of her crew including the Italian admiral, an act which was later blamed upon Austrian saboteurs, but was more likely an internal explosion. On December 11, 1916, *Regina Margherita* was sunk off Valona by mines laid by the successful German submarine minelayer *UC-14*.

ABOVE: **The high sides and massive central superstructure on 13,209 tonnes/13,000 tons displacement showing perhaps some French design influence on *Regina Margherita*.** BELOW: **The ship's company lined up for their photograph.** BELOW LEFT: **A stern view of this fine ship in 1910. In profile they looked like full-grown battleships.**

Regina Margherita class

Class: *Regina Margherita, Benedetto Brin.*
  Launched 1901
Dimensions: Length – 130m/426ft 6in
  Beam – 23.8m/78ft 2in
  Draught – 8.8m/28ft 11in
Displacement: 13,427 tonnes/13,215 tons
Armament: Main – 4 x 305mm/12in and
  4 x 205mm/8in guns
  Secondary – 20 x 75mm/3in guns and
  4 x 450mm/17.7in torpedoes
Machinery: 28 boilers, 2 shafts.
  16,249kW/21,790ihp
Speed: 20 knots
Complement: 812 men

Regina Elena class

Vittorio Cuniberti succeeded Brin as the leading Italian ship designer and he was tasked with planning a ship with 12 205mm/8in guns, moderate armour and a speed of 22 knots. Cuniberti produced a design with two single 305mm/12in guns in addition to the required 12 205mm/8in guns.

Cuniberti was also first to produce a design for an all-big-gun battleship. However, such a ship was too ambitious for the Italian navy even given its record of innovation. Instead Cuniberti was given permission to publish an article abroad, and in 1903 *Jane's Fighting Ships* printed "An Ideal Battleship for the British Fleet", in which Cuniberti proposed a warship of 17,273 tonnes/ 17,000 tons armed with 12 305mm/12in

guns in single and double turrets, with 305mm/12in armour (which would certainly have been unusual for the Italian navy) and high speed of 24 knots. An article by Cuniberti three years earlier in *Marine Rundschau* entitled "*Ein neuer Schlachtschifftypus*" had gone unnoticed. However, his *Jane's* article was read in London just when the British Admiralty, where Jacky Fisher was First Sea Lord, was considering the lessons learned from the Battle of Tsushima and the design of its next generation of battleships. It is therefore clear that Cuniberti's ideas contributed to the design for Dreadnought.

Meanwhile in Italy, Cuniberti's design for a battleship that was faster than any British or French ship and stronger than

any armoured cruiser became the successful Regina Elena class. Two ships were authorized in 1901 and two more the following year. They were elegant ships with fine lines and scalloped fore-ends to provide a forward arc of fire for the 205mm/8in guns which were all mounted in turrets, with a single turret-mounted 305mm/12in gun at each end, and three tall funnels, although these were later cut down with some positive effect on the ship's speed.

Regina Elena class	
Class: *Regina Elena, Vittorio Emanuele, Roma, Napoli*. Launched 1904–7	
Dimensions: Length – 132.6m/435ft	
Beam – 22.4m/73ft 6in	
Draught – 7.9m/25ft 11in	
Displacement: 12,751 tonnes/12,550 tons	
Armament: Main – 2 x 305mm/12in and	
12 x 205mm/8in guns	
Secondary – 16 x 75mm/3in guns and	
2 x 450mm/17.7in torpedoes	
Machinery: 28 boilers, 2 shafts.	
14,392kW/19,300ihp	
Speed: 22 knots	
Complement: 742 men	

LEFT: **The Regina Elena class was armed with two single 305mm/12in guns, mounted one forward and one aft.** BELOW LEFT: *Regina Elena, Roma* and *Napoli* **on manoeuvres off Venice in 1910.** BELOW: *Regina Elena* **at anchor at Messina in December 1908 after the earthquake there.**

Sissoi Veliki

The Russian navy built a number of powerful, and in some cases innovative, ironclad warships after the Russian War 1854–6. The Russians also participated in every stage of ship evolution from the screw line-of-battle ship, broadside and central battery ship, to the turret ship, coast defence monitor, and coast defence turret ship. They first put 300mm/12in guns in the turret ship *Petr Veliki* (1869) and in the circular coast defence ships *Novgorod* and *Vice Admiral Popov* in 1872–4, and this became the standard armament for successive classes of barbette and turret ships from then on.

In 1892 the Russian navy laid down its first battleship of the modern era at the New Admiralty yard in St Petersburg. *Sissoi Veliki* was a small ship for her armament, presumably intended for operations in the Baltic and to be the largest warship of any navy bordering on the Baltic coast, when the Swedes were still seen as the Russian navy's traditional enemies. However she had a high freeboard, was ocean-going and twice deployed from the Baltic to the Far East.

Sissoi Veliki suffered a serious accident in 1897 when one of her main guns fired before the breech was closed, but she was repaired in time to be part of the allied naval forces off China in 1900 during the Boxer Rebellion. The international fleet consisted of American, Austrian, British, French, German, Italian, Japanese and Russian ships under the command of the British admiral, Sir Edward Seymour. Seymour had landed sailors and marines to defend the embassies in Peking and these had become cut off. As part of the relief operations, the allied fleet bombarded the Taku forts at the entrance to the Peiho River and a squadron of ships forced their way upstream.

Sissoi Veliki's armoured belt was 405mm/16in to 305mm/12in thick and the turret armour 305mm/12in, which were to prove their worth at the Battle of Tsushima on May 27, 1905. She was one of six battleships lost there – the greatest number in any single battle of the steam age. The Russian pre-Dreadnoughts *Sevastapol, Kniaz Suvarov, Osliabia, Borodino, Imperator Alexander III* and

ABOVE: **A picture from the British Admiralty files dated 1910 of** *Sissoi Veliki.* **Despite the small size of these ships, Russian designers managed to fit them with two double turrets.** *Sissoi Veliki* **also made two voyages to the Far East, though on the second occasion to defeat at the Battle of Tsushima.**

Navarin were sunk by Japanese guns and torpedoes. *Sissoi Veliki* was hit by about 12 large-calibre shells, suffered serious bow damage near the waterline and was torpedoed in the stern, but did not sink until her crew scuttled her.

Sissoi Veliki

Class: *Sissoi Veliki.* Launched 1894
Dimensions: Length – 107.2m/351ft 10in
  Beam – 20.7m/68ft in
  Draught – 7.8m/25ft 6in
Displacement: 10,567 tonnes/10,400 tons
Armament: Main – 4 x 305mm/12in and
  6 x 150mm/6in guns
  Secondary – 12 x 3pdr, 18 x 1pdr guns and
  6 x 455mm/18in torpedoes
Machinery: 12 Belleville boilers, 2 shafts,
  6,400kW/8,500ihp
Speed: 16 knots
Complement: 586 men

Admiral Ushakov class

The Admiral Ushakov class were built as part of a Baltic naval arms race, and in particular to counter the Swedish coast defence ships of the Svea and Oden classes. Mounting four 255mm/10in guns on a displacement of under 5,080 tonnes/5,000 tons (and 15 per cent overweight compared to their design) they were hardly suitable for a voyage to the Pacific in 1904–5, although some sources say that these ships were good sea-keepers.

The three ships differed slightly: *Admiral Seniavin* was the heaviest ship and drew more water, while *Admiral General Graf Apraksin* had only one gun fitted in the after turret. The armour on all three ships was only 150mm/6in to 230mm/9in thick.

The gun was unsuccessful: designed for the Russian army and navy, both to be fitted in ships and mounted in coastal batteries, the naval version was too lightly constructed, suffered from weak barrels and thus had poor ballistic qualities. The land version had better ballistic qualities but it had primitive

mountings which restricted its rate of fire. Nevertheless four guns were mounted in the Black Sea battleship *Rostislav* in 1898. The Russian army had a battery of these guns at Port Arthur by 1904, and they became the main coast defence guns of the Russian navy until World War I.

At the Battle of Tsushima in 1905 *Admiral Ushakov* fought bravely. She was hit twice below the waterline and once above by Japanese heavy shells, and was left behind by the Russian fleet. The next day, May 28, out of ammunition and surrounded by Japanese armoured cruisers, *Admiral Ushakov* was scuttled by her own crew.

Admiral Seniavin was badly damaged on May 27 and surrendered to the Japanese the next day. Renamed

BELOW: **The proportions of** *General Admiral Graf Apraksin* **make her look like a lake steamer. She was not designed for the oceanic voyage to the Battle at Tsushima in 1905.** RIGHT: *Admiral Seniavin* **at speed. The clouds of smoke reveal the logistic and strategic weakness of these coal-burners.**

Admiral Ushakov class

Class: *Admiral Ushakov, Admiral Seniavin, General Admiral Graf Apraksin.* Launched 1893–6
Dimensions: Length – 87.3m/286ft 6in
 Beam – 15.85m/52ft
 Draught – 5.9m/19ft 6in
Displacement: 5,051 tonnes/4,971 tons
Armament: Main – 4 x 255mm/10in and
 4 x 120mm/4.7in guns
 Secondary – 6 x 3pdr, 10 x 1pdr guns and
 4 x 380mm/15in torpedoes
Machinery: 8 boilers, 2 shafts, 4,288kW/5,750ihp
Speed: 16 knots
Complement: 404 men

Mishima, she remained in service with the Imperial Japanese Navy until 1928. *General Admiral Graf Apraksin* also surrendered, and served as the *Okinoshima* until being scrapped in 1926.

Petropavlovsk class

Named after important Russian victories on land, the Petropavlovsk class were flush-decked ships with an appreciable tumblehome. Like earlier Russian battleships they were overweight, in this case by about 10 per cent compared to their design. However, they followed what had now become a standard pattern with twin 305mm/12in turrets, one forward, one aft. Eight of the 150mm/6in guns were mounted in turrets and four in a central battery, port and starboard. Like earlier Russian ships they were seemingly well armoured with belts tapering from 305mm/12in to 205mm/8in thick.

All three ships formed part of the Russian First Pacific Squadron based at Port Arthur and were there at the outbreak of the Russo-Japanese War. *Petropavlovsk* struck a mine and blew up on April 13, 1904, with heavy loss of life including the Commander-in-Chief of the Russian Pacific Fleet, Admiral Makarov.

The other ships of the class proved to be much more resilient. At the Battle of the Yellow Sea on August 10, 1904, *Poltava* survived being hit by over a dozen rounds of 305mm/12in and

205mm/8in shells. She was hit again at the siege of Port Arthur with howitzer shells fired by the Japanese army, caught fire and sank. She was raised by the Japanese and commissioned as the *Tango*. In 1916 she was sold back to the Russians and this time named *Tchesma* (the name *Poltava* having already been taken for a Russian Dreadnought-type) and sent to the White Sea. *Sevastopol* was also mined on June 23, 1904, and again on August 23, 1904, but survived both incidents. She sustained several hits during the Battle of the Yellow Sea, and at the siege of Port Arthur, after being hit five times by 280mm/11in shells, sallied from the harbour. Her captain, Essen, took her to a new anchorage outside the harbour but close inshore and there, behind boom defences, she survived nightly attack for seven nights in December 1904 by Japanese torpedo boats. Three torpedoes exploded in her

nets without causing much damage to *Sevastopol*, but a fourth torpedo hit her stern. On January 2, 1905, Essen had *Sevastopol* towed into deep water where he scuttled her.

The Russian ships in the Far East were generally courageously fought, and proved themselves capable of sustaining much damage. The Russian fleet owed its defeats, through the Russo-Japanese War, more to the lack of logistic support than to a want of bravery, until by 1905 morale had also begun to collapse.

Petropavlovsk class

Class: *Petropavlovsk, Poltava, Sevastopol.*
  Launched 1894–5
Dimensions: Length – 112.5m/369ft
  Beam – 21.3m/70ft
  Draught – 7.8m/25ft 6in
Displacement: 11,536 tonnes/11,354 tons
Armament: Main – 4 x 305mm/12in and
  12 x 150mm/6in guns
  Secondary – 12 x 3pdr, 28 x 1pdr guns,
  6 x 455mm/18in torpedoes and 60 mines
Machinery: 12 boilers, 2 shafts,
  8,389kW/11,250ihp
Speed: 16.5 knots
Complement: 632 men

BELOW: ***Petropavlovsk*** **and her two sisters formed the Russian First Pacific Squadron and were in the Far East when the Russo-Japanese war broke out. Despite their limitations they fought bravely but were inevitably overwhelmed by the Japanese.**

Rostislav

The battleship *Rostislav*, laid down in 1894, is notable for being the first oil-fired battleship in the world, although she was also capable of burning coal. Originally intended to be a copy of the *Sissoi Veliki*, she was supplied with rather unsatisfactory 255mm/10in guns and the Nicolaiev yard on the Black Sea made other changes. Constructed to the same length as *Sissoi Veliki* she emerged with two turrets in the contemporary layout, but with an extra two 205mm/8in guns in the central battery. She also displaced about 1,524 tonnes/1,500 tons less than *Sissoi Veliki*. Although slow and weak, she saw plenty of action in World War I.

Learning the lessons of the Battle of Tsushima, the Russian Black Sea battleship squadron was formed into a single firing-unit of 305mm/12in-gunned ships, from which *Rostislav* was excluded. The fall of her 255mm/10in rounds were so different from the larger shells of the other battleships, and potentially confusing to the fire controller, that she was actually forbidden from firing tactically on the same target.

However, as early as November 1914 *Rostislav* was used to bombard Turkish shore facilities at Zonguldak, and she was present at the first action of World War I when battleships engaged each other. As the Russian Black Sea fleet was returning to Sevastopol on November 18, it was intercepted by the German-manned and Turkish-flagged *Goeben* and *Breslau*. While *Goeben* duelled with the battleship *Evstafi* and her sisters, *Rostislav* engaged the *Breslau* and drove her to the disengaged side of *Goeben*.

Rostislav returned several times in 1915 to bombard facilities and prohibit sea traffic on the south coast of Turkey, and in 1916 she was employed supporting the Russian troops in the Caucasus. On September 2, 1916, while at anchor in the Romanian port of Constanta, she was hit by a bomb dropped from a German seaplane.

At the end of the war *Rostislav* was captured alongside by advancing armies under German command, but retaken by British and French forces supporting the Whites during the Russian revolution.

ABOVE: **In theory the Black Sea in World War I should have been dominated by the German battlecruiser *Goeben*, but the Russian Black Sea Fleet of pre-Dreadnoughts were well handled and were able to operate widely throughout the theatre.**

Her internal machinery had been wrecked, so in November 1920 *Rostislav* was grounded off Kerch as a fixed battery. *Rostislav* survived until 1930 when she was broken up, being the last surviving battleship of the Imperial Russian Navy.

Rostislav

Class: *Rostislav*. Launched 1896
Dimensions: Length – 107.2m/351ft 10in
 Beam – 20.73m/68ft
 Draught - 6.7m/22ft
Displacement: 9,022 tonnes/8,880 tons
Armament: Main – 4 x 255mm/10in and
 8 x 150mm/6in guns
 Secondary – 20 x 3pdr guns and
 6 x 455mm/18in torpedoes
Machinery: 12 boilers, 2 shafts.
 6,488kW/8,700ihp
Speed: 16 knots
Complement: 650 men

Peresviet class

The Peresviet class with their three funnels, length and extended forecastle deck, and French-style tumblehome, French-type turrets, weak armament and miserable speed were thoroughly unsatisfactory. Besides two twin 255mm/10in turrets they had five 150mm/6in guns in casemates port and starboard and a bow chaser. The *Peresviet* and *Osliabia* were built by the New Admiralty yard in St Petersburg and *Pobieda* was built by the Baltic Works in St Petersburg and incorporated some minor changes. The main belt of armour, Russian-made "Harvey-ized" in the first units, and steel alloy in *Pobieda,* was 95m/312ft long and 2.44m/8ft deep.

Peresviet was seriously damaged at the Battle of the Yellow Sea. The Japanese captured a hill overlooking Port Arthur and used it to spot the fall of shot of the advancing army's 280mm/11in howitzers. *Peresviet* was hit by at least 23 rounds and was scuttled on December 7, 1904.

The Japanese raised her and named her *Sagami*. In 1916 Russia needed warships to guard her White Sea ports against the Germans and *Sagami* was repurchased and given back her old name. However, she ran aground off Vladivostok on May 26, 1916, and stuck fast for two months. Then on January 4, 1917, *Peresviet* struck a mine laid by the German minelayer *U-73* and sank 16km/10 miles from Port Said, this time for good. Few ships can claim to have been sunk twice.

Osliabia was in the Baltic when the Russo-Japanese war broke out, and was sent to the Far East as part of the Russian Second Pacific Squadron. She was sunk by gunfire at the Battle of Tsushima. During the Russo-Japanese War *Pobieda* struck a mine on April 13, 1904, but the force of the explosion was

largely absorbed by a coal bunker and she was repaired in time to be present at the Battle of the Yellow Sea in August 1904. She was finally sunk on December 7, 1904, at Port Arthur. Despite 21 280mm/11in howitzer hits, the Japanese were able to raise her and bring her into service as the *Suwo*. She was finally scrapped in 1922.

BELOW: *Pobieda* **was mined in 1904 and heavily shelled at Port Arthur. However, she was raised and served on as the Japanese** *Suwo* **until 1922.**

Peresviet class

Class: *Peresviet, Osliabia, Pobieda.* Launched 1898–1900
Dimensions: Length – 132.3m/434ft
Beam – 21.8m/71ft 6in
Draught – 7.9m/26ft
Displacement: 12,887 tonnes/12,683 tons
Armament: Main – 4 x 255mm/10in and 11 x 150mm/6in guns
Secondary – 20 x 11pdr, 20 x 3pdr, 8 x 1pdr guns and 5 x 380mm/15in torpedoes
Machinery: 32 Belleville boilers, 3 shafts. 11,186kW/15,000ihp
Speed: 18 knots
Complement: 752 men

LEFT: **The battleship *Potemkin*, also known under other names, was made famous by Sergei Eisenstein's classic black and white film of the 1905 mutiny onboard which presaged the Russian Revolution. Although she may have flown as many as five different national flags, it is as *Potemkin* that she will always be known.**

Potemkin

The pre-Dreadnought *Kniaz Potemkin Tavricheski* is universally known as the battleship *Potemkin* and for the mutiny which took place aboard on June 25, 1905. Following "Bloody Sunday", when Cossacks had savagely suppressed a protest march on the Winter Palace in St Petersburg on January 22, 1905, the Black Sea port of Odessa remained calm until strikes were called that spring. Socialists had been agitating in the fleet since 1903, but *Potemkin* was regarded as one of the most loyal of ships. However, a mutiny was planned during gunnery exercises, the eventual cause being a refusal to eat maggot-infested meat. *Potemkin*'s captain assured his men that the meat was edible while his second-in-command threatened to shoot 12 sailors chosen at random. There were shouts, small arms were seized and within a few minutes seven officers had been killed and their bodies thrown over the side.

A People's Committee took the ship to Odessa, where the mutineers threatened to bombard the city. However, after several hundred pro-mutiny demonstrators were massacred by Cossacks near the Richelieu Steps,

Potemkin's guns remained silent because the mutineers did not know who to fire on. That night rioting broke out and some 6,000 people were killed by soldiers and looters.

When the barbette ships *Georgi Pobiedonsets* and *Dvenadtsat Apostolov*, and the turret ship *Tri Sviatitelia* approached Odessa, *Potemkin* ordered them to "Surrender or we fire" and the Russian admiral retired to join his commander-in-chief at Tendra Island. When the squadron returned, reinforced by the battleship *Rostislav* and the barbette ship *Sinop*, *Potemkin* steamed out again and this time the barbette ship *Georgi Pobiedonsets* surrendered to mutineers onboard and returned to Odessa with the *Potemkin*.

Over the summer the mutiny subsided and *Potemkin* took refuge in nearby Constanta, Romania, where she was scuttled in shallow water and the crew stole away. By July 11, *Potemkin* had been pumped out and towed back into Russian waters. The mutiny that foreshadowed the Russian Revolution by 12 years was over. In October the Tsar exorcised *Potemkin*'s black history by renaming her *Pantelimon*, and she saw

service in World War I until in April 1917 the Provisional Government renamed her *Potemkin* and, a month later, *Boretz zu Svobodu*. She changed hands several times as independence-seeking Ukrainians, the German army, and counter-revolutionaries occupied Sevastopol. While the British temporarily held Sevastopol, men from the cruiser *Calypso* disabled her engines on April 25, 1919, and in November 1920 the Red Army finally seized control.

Potemkin, immortalized in Sergei Eisenstein's classic silent film *Battleship Potemkin*, was broken up in 1922.

Potemkin

Class: *Kniaz Potemkin Tavricheski.* Launched 1900
Dimensions: Length – 115.4m/378ft 6in
  Beam – 22.25m/73ft
  Draught – 8.2m/27ft
Displacement: 12,784 tonnes/12,582 tons
Armament: Main – 4 x 305mm/12in and
  16 x 150mm/6in guns
  Secondary – 14 x 11pdr guns and
  5 x 380mm/15in torpedoes
Machinery: 22 Belleville boilers, 2 shafts,
  7,904kW/10,600ihp
Speed: 16.5 knots
Complement: 750 men

LEFT: *Retvisan*, another Russian ship which was fought bravely and survived the Russo-Japanese War until sunk by the besieging artillery.

Retvisan

These two similar ships were ordered from foreign yards as the Imperial Russian Navy built up its three fleets, in the Baltic, the Black Sea and the Pacific. *Retvisan* was a three-funnelled, flush-deck ship, while the *Tsessarevitch*, though similar in length and displacement, had two funnels and her pronounced tumblehome gave away her French origins. They had similar main armament, but *Retvisan*'s 150mm/6in guns were mounted four in casemates and eight in a main deck battery. *Tsessarevitch* had her 150mm/6in guns in turrets and she was slightly more heavily armoured. Undoubtedly they were the best Russian battleships to date, and they were sent to join the Russian fleet based at Port Arthur. There they were joined by the battleships *Petropavlovsk*, *Poltava*, *Sevastopol*, *Pobieda* and *Peresviet* as well as many cruisers, gunboats and auxiliaries.

Retvisan

Class: *Retvisan*. Launched 1900

Dimensions: Length – 117.9m/386ft 8in
Beam – 22.2m/72ft 8in
Draught – 7.9m/26ft

Displacement: 13,107 tonnes/12,900 tons

Armament: Main – 4 x 305mm/12in and
12 x 150mm/6in guns
Secondary – 20 x 11pdr, 24 x 11pdr, 24 x 2pdr,
8 x 1pdr guns 6 x 380mm/15in torpedoes
and 45 mines

Machinery: 24 Niclausse boilers, 2 shafts,
12,677kW/17,000ihp

Speed: 18 knots

Complement: 738 men

Tsessarevitch

LEFT: **Tsessarevitch**, onboard which the Russian Admiral Vitgeft lost his life when a Japanese shell struck the bridge during the Battle of the Yellow Sea in August 1904.

Tsessarevitch

Class: *Tsessarevitch*. Launched 1901

Dimensions: Length – 118.5m/388ft 9in
Beam – 23.2m/76ft 1in
Draught – 7.9m/26ft

Displacement: 13,122 tonnes/12,915 tons

Armament: Main – 4 x 305mm/12in,
12 x 150mm/6in guns
Secondary – 20 x 11pdr, 20 x 3pdr guns,
4 x 380mm/15in torpedoes and 45 mines

Machinery: 20 Belleville boilers, 2 shafts,
12,304kW/16,500ihp

Speed: 18.5 knots

Complement: 782 men

Japan broke diplomatic relations with Russia on February 6, 1904, and two Russian ships were sunk at sea on February 8, although war was not declared when on February 8 and 9, Japanese destroyers attempted to "Copenhagen" the Russian ships in Port Arthur, which was un-expecting and gaily lit. Of 20 torpedoes fired, two reached *Retvisan* and *Tsessarevitch*, which ran aground, though both were soon raised and repaired. Despite its disorder the *Tsessarevitch* steamed out the next day to thwart a major Japanese attack.

Later, when the fleets met on August 10, 1904, in the Battle of the Yellow Sea, both sides concentrated fire on the head of the other's line, the battleships *Mikasa* and *Tsessarevitch* respectively. A dozen 305mm/12in rounds crashed into *Tsessarevitch*, killing Rear Admiral Vitgeft and hitting the control tower, causing *Tsessarevitch* to veer out of control. She was later interned in Kiao Chau, a German concession on the Chinese coast.

Retvisan was also hit nearly a score of times but managed to return to Port Arthur where she was besieged with the rest of the Russian fleet and sunk by howitzers of the Japanese army on December 6, 1904. She was raised and repaired by the Japanese navy and commissioned as the *Hizen*, the only American-built battleship in the steam age to be captured by an enemy or to have flown two flags. She was sunk as a target in 1924.

In World War I, *Tsessarevitch* served in the Baltic and was engaged by the German Dreadnought *Kronprinz* on October 17, 1917, but escaped with only two hits. She was scrapped in 1922.

Borodino class

The five battleships of the Borodino class took the *Tsessarevitch* as their model. However, post-battle analysis of the Russo-Japanese war revealed some serious flaws in the French design. The class had a very pronounced tumblehome, with the hull sides curved sharply inward from the waterline, and they proved to be extraordinarily manoeuvrable, but under certain conditions of flooding the centre of gravity of these ships could change rapidly. This created instability and a large overturning momentum, just as the French battleship, *Bouvet,* demonstrated when she capsized after striking a mine off the Dardanelles in March 1915.

Previous Russian warships, whatever their defects, stood up well to battle damage, and the Borodinos, though their armoured belt was thinner and narrower than in the *Tsessarevitch* prototype, also sustained a great deal of damage before four of them succumbed at the Battle of Tsushima.

Borodino, Imperator Alexander III, Orel and *Kniaz Suvarov* were all at the Battle of Tsushima and in theory these modern ships should have acquitted themselves

well, but material weaknesses and perhaps human exhaustion made these an ill-fated group of ships. The Russians fought their ships hard, but as *Kniaz Suvarov* led the line she became the first target for the Japanese gunners. When her steering gear was damaged, she was forced out of line, and repeatedly hit by shellfire, torpedoed and sank.

Imperator Alexander III took the lead but was soon enveloped in flames and began to list heavily from a hit in the bows. This caused flooding and she later capsized. *Borodino*'s end was even quicker and more dramatic: she suffered a magazine explosion and blew up.

Orel's superstructure was badly damaged and although she survived the day, she surrendered the following day. Once repaired, *Orel* served the Japanese as *Iwami* until being scrapped in 1922.

Only the last ship of the class, *Slava*, was not ready and so did not sail for the Far East. In World War I she fought the German Dreadnought *König* off Moon Sound in the Gulf of Riga on October 17, 1917, when she flooded so much that she grounded and was scuttled by torpedo. The wreck was broken up in 1935.

ABOVE: **The Borodino class was a successful development of *Tsessarevitch* and their presence gave some homogeneity to the Russian line at the Battle of Tsushima. Only *Slava* was not ready in time to steam to the Far East, but she gave a good account of herself in the Baltic in World War I. At Tsushima *Borodino*, seen here, blew up after a shell hit a magazine. *Slava*, a sister ship, had more success against a German Dreadnought in World War I, but ran aground and was sunk by her own side.**

Borodino class

Class: *Borodino, Imperator Alexander III, Orel, Kniaz Suvarov, Slava.* Launched 1901–3
Dimensions: Length – 121m/397ft
Beam – 23.2m/76ft 2in
Draught – 8m/26ft 2in
Displacement: 13,733 tonnes/13,516 tons
Armament: Main – 4 x 305mm/12in and
12 x 150mm/6in guns
Secondary – 20 x 11pdr, 20 x 3pdr guns and
4 x 380mm/15in torpedoes
Machinery: 20 Belleville boilers, 2 shafts,
12,155kW/16,300ihp
Speed: 18 knots
Complement: 835 men

LEFT: **The Russians learned valuable lessons from the Battle of Tsushima and when they next faced battle *Evstafi* and *Ioann Zlatoust* acquitted themselves well.**

Evstafi class

G enerally similar to *Potemkin* and laid down in 1898, these two ships spent some time on the slips while the Russians considered the lessons of the Russo-Japanese War. As a result their armour was improved, especially to the upper deck which was increased to 205mm/8in. The trend towards larger guns was followed and the Evstafis were fitted with 205mm/8in guns. Later in World War I they were also fitted with additional anti-aircraft guns.

The Russian navy as a whole learned other lessons from the Russo-Japanese War, and the Russians developed a system whereby the centre ship of a squadron of three would control the fire of all ships. Equipment and procedures for transmitting the range and correction data between ships were devised and the range-tables for all major guns were revised. New shells with more reliable and predictable trajectories were designed and gun mountings improved,

including smoke-extraction fans to keep the turrets clear. With these gunnery improvements and more thorough training, *Evstafi* and *Ioann Zlatoust* formed the core of a squadron which acquitted itself well when it came up against the more recent *Goeben*.

Evstafi class

Class: *Evstafi, Ioann Zlatoust.* Launched 1906
Dimensions: Length – 118m/387ft 3in
   Beam – 22.6m/74ft
   Draught – 8.2m/27ft
Displacement: 13,046 tonnes/12,840 tons
Armament: Main – 4 x 305mm/12in,
   4 x 205mm/8in and 12 x 150mm/6in guns
   Secondary – 14 x 11pdr and 6 x 3pdr guns and
   3 x 455mm/18in torpedoes
Machinery: 22 Belleville boilers, 2 shafts,
   8,054kW/10,800ihp
Speed: 16.5 knots
Complement: 879 men

Imperator Pavel class

LEFT: **The last pre-Dreadnoughts of the Russian navy seen at anchor together in the Baltic.**

T hese were the last pre-Dreadnoughts to be built for the Imperial Russian navy and showed all the lessons of the Russo-Japanese war. A large number of 205mm/8in secondary guns were mounted in turrets and casemates, and the hulls were completely armoured – even to the removal of scuttles and

deadlights. Originally fitted with slender US-style cage or lattice masts, these were cut down to funnel height and replaced with pole masts. They took little part in the Baltic fighting in World War I.

Imperator Pavel, renamed *Respublika* in 1917, was scrapped in 1923. *Andrei Peroswanni* was torpedoed in Kronstadt

harbour on August 18, 1919, long after the war in the rest of Europe was over, during an attack by British coastal motorboats. She was scrapped in 1925.

Imperator Pavel class

Class: *Imperator Pavel, Andrei Peroswanni.*
   Launched 1906–7
Dimensions: Length – 140.2m/460ft
   Beam – 24.4m/80ft
   Draught – 8.2m/27ft
Displacement: 17,679 tonnes/17,400 tons
Armament: Main – 4 x 305mm/12in,
   14 x 205mm/8in and 12 x 120mm/4.7in guns
   Secondary – 4 x 3pdr guns and
   3 x 455mm/18in torpedoes
Machinery: 22 Belleville boilers, 2 shafts,
   13,423kW/18,000ihp
Speed: 17.5 knots
Complement: 933men

LEFT: **Austro-Hungarian naval architects had some help from their German-speaking cousins, but generally their designs were their own. The Habsburg class were small, well-proportioned vessels.**

Habsburg class

Austro-Hungarian provinces in the northern and eastern Adriatic Sea gave the otherwise landlocked empire access to the sea. From the mid-1800s a significant navy was developed, modelled on British lines, and the first ship was a steam frigate ordered from England at the end of the Russian War 1854–6. The first torpedoes were designed and built in Austria, and the Austro-Hungarian navy distinguished itself in fighting the Danes in the North Sea in support of their allies the

Prussians in 1866. The empire, however, had a continental outlook and the navy was starved of funds. Nevertheless, the Austro-Hungarians, although often building only single ships, took part in the development of the battleship from broadside ironclad to centre-battery ship and coast defence ships, sometimes mounting quite large guns.

The three units of the Habsburg class are listed here because, though their guns were less than 255mm/10in, they were heavily armoured, seagoing and

had a significant impact upon the regional balance of power. Although modified before the war, when the superstructure of *Habsburg* was reduced by one deck, they were obsolete by 1914, when Austro-Hungary fought Italy. Although used on isolated operations, as when *Babenburg* shelled the Italian port of Ancona in 1915, by the end of the war their crews had been drafted into the submarine and air services. All three were ceded to Britain in 1920 and scrapped in Italy in 1921.

Erzherzog Karl class

LEFT: **The Erzherzog Karl class was a successful design for a small pre-Dreadnought. Like other ships then building on the slips, they were made obsolescent by the launch of *Dreadnought*. In World War I they were used for bombardment.**

These were the three largest and last pre-Dreadnoughts of the Austro-Hungarian navy. Like previous designs, they were compact ships, limited by the size of the dockyard facilities at Trieste, though compared to their Italian rivals they were better armoured. They also displayed some advances, and for the first time the secondary guns in their casemates were electrically operated.

Launched in 1903–5, however, the class was rendered obsolete while the ships were being completed by the launch in Portsmouth of *Dreadnought*.

During World War I they were limited to the role of shore bombardment, including a raid on May 24, 1915, on the city and ancient ferry port of Ancona. In early 1918 they were used in helping to suppress a mutiny at Cattaro.

At the end of the war all three ships were seized at Pola by the newly independent state of Yugoslavia, but *Erzherzog Karl* and *Erzherzog Friedrich* were ceded to France and *Erzherzog Ferdinand Max* to Britain, but all were broken up in 1920/1.

Glossary

Aft — at or towards the rear or stern

Armourclad — *see* ironclad

Barbette — originally, the open-topped armoured enclosure from which a gun was fired; later, the standing or fixed part of the gun mounting, protecting the hoists and connecting the turret to the magazines

Battle cruiser — ship armed with battleship-sized guns, but in which armour has been dispensed with for speed and manoeuvrability

Beam — the widest part of a ship

Bilge — the lowest part of the hull of a ship, where the side turns into the bottom

Bilge keel — fins or narrow wings at the turn of the bilge, designed to improve stability

Blister — *see* bulge

Block ship — a battleship converted into a floating battery intended to defend habours

Bow — (or bows) the forward end of a ship

Breastwork — raised armoured bulkhead to protect a gun and its moving parts

Bulge — (or blister) a longitudinal space, subdivided and filled with fuel, water or air, to protect against the effects of a torpedo hit

Bulkhead — the internal vertical structures within a ship

Calibre — the internal diameter or bore of a gun, or the ratio of the barrel length to the bore

Capital ship — a generic name given to the largest and most powerful ships in a navy

Casemate — an armoured box or battery in which one or usually more guns were mounted

Cofferdam — watertight bulkhead separating and protecting magazines and engine rooms

ABOVE: **A detail of the bow decoration of *New Hampshire* taken while in dry dock.**

Copenhagen — reference to the British attack on the Danish capital and fleet in 1807

Dressed overall — a ship dressed *en fête*, flying lines of flags between her masts, when not underway

Dwarf bulkhead — low bulkhead intended to stop the free flood of water

Flotilla — a squadron in the Royal Navy before NATO standardization

Flying deck — a deck suspended between two parts of the superstructure so that the deck below can be kept clear for mounting guns

Forecastle — forward part of a ship

Freeboard — height of the deck above the waterline

Great White Fleet — USN fleet that circumnavigated the globe to demonstrate the coming-of-age of the USA as a sea power

Gunwales — upper edge of the side of a vessel

Heel — lean or tilt of a ship

Ihp — indicated horsepower: the calculated output of a ship's machinery

Ironclad — a ship protected by vertical iron plating

Laid down — reference to when a new ship was first placed on the construction slip

Line ahead — when ships form up in a line

Line-of-battle ship — a ship large enough to be in the line

LEFT: **A close-up of the 305mm/12in gun mounting in *Ohio*.**

Metacentre	roll and return to upright slowly
Monitor	low freeboard coast defence vessel
Ordnance	armament and ammunition of a ship
Pole mast	a stick-like mast to carry aerials or flags
Port	left side
Quarter	between the beam and the stern
Ram	underwater beak or spur on the bow for striking the enemy
Screw	propellor
Shp	shaft horse power: the actual measured output of a ship's machinery
Starboard	right side
Stern	rear of a ship
Theatre	the area in which a ship or fleet operates or a naval campaign takes place
Tripod mast	a mast having extra legs to carry the weight of direction-finding and gunnery control positions
Tumblehome	inward curve of a ship's side above the waterline
Turret	revolving armoured gun house
USN	United States Navy
Van	the front of a formation of ships

Key to flags

For the specification boxes, the national flag that was current at the time of the ship's use is shown.

 Austro-Hungary

Britain

France

Germany

 Italy

Japan

Russia

 USA

BELOW: **A ship belonging to the Danton class, which had large calibre secondary armaments.**

Acknowledgements

The publisher would like to thank the following individuals and picture libraries for the use of their pictures in the book. Every effort has been made to acknowledge the pictures properly, however we apologize if there are any unintentional omissions, which will be corrected in future editions.

l=left, r=right, t=top, b=bottom, m=middle, lm= lower middle

Alinari Archives-Florence: 80m (Touring Club Italiano); 80b; 81m (De Pinto Donazione); 81bl; 81br Malandrini Ferruccio);

Australian War Memorial: 37tl (P00952.003);

Cody Images: 6t; 6m; 7tr; 7mr; 7bl; 8–9; 10t; 10bl; 11; 12m; 13t; 13b; 14bl; 14br; 15br; 16t; 16mr; 17tr; 17b; 18t; 18m; 19t; 19ml; 19mr; 22t; 22b; 23; 24t; 24m; 25t; 25b; 30b; 31t; 31mr; 32t; 33t; 33mr; 33br; 36; 37m; 38br; 39bl; 39br; 40mr; 40b; 41t; 41m; 42tl; 42br; 43; 44tl; 50tl; 50bl; 52t; 52b; 53t; 53b; 54t; 56t; 56m; 56mr; 57tl; 57tr; 57mr; 58mr; 59m; 59bl; 59br; 60tl; 60tr; 60mr; 61m; 61bl; 62mr; 64t; 64b; 65t; 66t; 66b; 67t; 67b; 69t; 69m; 69b; 74t; 74m; 75t; 75m; 75b; 76t; 76b; 77ml; 77mr; 77b; 78tr; 79t; 80t; 82t; 83m; 83b; 87t; 88t; 89t; 90t; 90b; 92t; 92b; 93; 94t; 94b; 95t; 95b; 96t; 96b.

Imperial War Museum Photograph Archive: 12b (Q22212); 15t (Q40607); 38t (Q41317); 42tr (Q22284); 68t (Q22357); 70t (Q22258); 70bl (Q41314); 71t (Q22279); 71mr (Q13412); 78tl (Q41298); 78mr (Q41285); 79b (Q19930); 86 (Q22446); 88b (Q41361); 91t (Q70143); 91b (Q70145).

Library of Congress: 21tl.

Mary Evans Picture Library: 28

National Archive of Scotland: 65m (UCS 1/116/4).

Novosti: 85t.

Curt Ohlsson: 37tr.

Royal Naval Museum: 44br; 45m; 45b; 46mr; 46bl; 47t; 47mr; 48tl; 48tr; 48m; 49t; 49mr; 50tr; 51tl; 51tr; 51m.

Erwin Sieche: 17m.

Topfoto: 65mr.

US Naval Historical Center: 20tr; 21mr; 24t; 24m; 29t; 29mr; 31b; 54bl; 55mr; 55b; 58tl; 59br; 61br; 62t; 68mr.

Walker Archive: 72tr; 72mr; 72bl; 73t; 73b.

ABOVE: **A British ship in dry dock.**
BOTTOM: *Missouri*

Index

ABOVE: **Nebraska, during speed trials, before acceptance into the USN.**

BELOW: **Illinois in dry dock in New Orleans Navy Yard in 1902.**

ABOVE: *Hatsuse* at her launch on June 27, 1899.

BOTTOM: The Russian battleship *Potemkin*.